HUMANIST WORDSWORTH

HUMANIST WORDSWORTH

(A Study of Humanism in his Major Poetry)

PRALAY KANT

Humanist Wordsworth : A Study of Humanism in his Major Poetry

Rs. 540

ISBN: 978-7835-762-1

Published in 2009 in India by
Kalpaz Publications
C-30, Satyawati Nagar,
Delhi-110052
E-mail: kalpaz@hotmail.com
Phone : 9212729499

Lasser Type Setting by: Rudra Computer Graphics, Delhi
Printed at : G. Print Process, Delhi

To my late brother

Ajju

(Mr. Ajay Kant Shrivastava)

Contents

	Preface	9
	Acknowledgments	11
1.	**Introduction**	15
2.	**Humanism in English Poetry : From Renaissance to Romantics**	37
3.	**Humanism in the Lyrical Ballads : 1798**	55
4.	**Humanism in the Lyrical Ballads : 1800**	81
5	**Humanism in the Selected Shorter Poems of Wordsworth**	97
6.	**Humanism in the Prelude**	123
7.	**Humanism in the Excursion**	163
8.	**Postscript : Wordsworth as a Bolshevist**	179
	Appendices	
	Appendix – I – Contents of The 1798 Edition of the Lyrical Vallads	185
	Appendix – II - Contents of The 1800 Edition of the Lyrical Vallads	187
	Appendix – III- Advertisement To Lyrical Ballads: 1798	191
	Bibliography	193
	Index	199

Preface

"Humanist Wordsworth" is essentially based on my Ph.D thesis "Humanism of William Wordsworth in his Major Poems" but I have analysed some more poets and added ideas which were not there in the thesis.

Wordsworth's poems such as "Intimations of Immortality from Recollections of the Early Childhood" and "Lines Composed A Few Miles Above Tintern, Abbey", which are generally prescribed for literature courses in English in Indian Universities are usually taken as examples of his spiritual inclinations, whereas in my opinion the real interest in Wordsworth's poetry lies in his humanism, as seen in Wordsworth's major Poems including those of the Lyrical Ballads (1798), The Prelude (1850) and Collection of poems published in 1805, 1807, 1815, 1819 and 1822. These poems evince not only Wordsworth's humanitarianism but also two other kinds of humanism-the Renaissance humanism and the Enlightenment humanism. This book is an attempt to bring to the notice of a scholar of English literature, the presence of different kinds of humanism in the major poetry of Wordsworth.

I hope this book ushers a reader of Wordsworth to a better understanding of his poetry and hopefully one ballad from the Lyrical Ballads will be introduced to the student of literature where it is not already prescribed.

975, South Civil Lines,
Pralay Kant
Jabalpur
Date:- 22-01-09

Acknowledgements

I will always be greatly indebted to Dr. (Mrs.) Urbashi Barat, My Ph.D Supervisor, Prof. and Head of the Department of Post-Graduate Studies and Research in English, Rani Durgavati Vishwavidyalaya, Jabalpur for her invaluable guidance in correcting and improving my thesis.

I also wish to express my thanks to my colleagues in the Department of English, Government Mahakoshal (Autonomous) Arts and Commerce College, Jabalpur, particularly Prof. (Mrs.) Apara Tiwari, Head of the Department for taking a keen interest in my work, Asst. Profs. (Mrs.) Meena Kellar and Mrs. Samata Naidu for providing me books without which it would have been impossible to accomplish this book and Dr. Deepak Shrivastava, Asst. Prof. in Political Science in my college, for suggesting me philosophical works of Bertrand Russell and Will Durant.

I am also grateful to various libraries of my college, specially Mr. Sharad Mathur, the Indo-American Information and Research Centre, Hyderabad and Gandhi Bhawan Library, Jabalpur. I also owe a debt to the libraries of the Depts. of English and Philosophy of Rani Durgavati Vishwavidyalaya Jabalpur.

I am grateful to my late father Shri Bhuvneshwari Pratap, for inculcating in me humanistic values without which I would not have thought of writing this book.

I am also thankful for my mother Mrs. Karuna Shrivastava's presence, which always motivated me to complete this book. This book would not have been possible had I not received support and cooperation from my wife, Mrs. Swastika Kant and my children Sahir and Gouri; I am also thankful to my brother-in-law Surg. Dr. Subodh Darbari and my sister Prof. Mrs. Mita Darbari for helping me out with the internet. I am also thankful to the enlightening discursions I had with my two young M.A. scholars, Mr. Manish Sharma and Mr. Vijendra Tiwari. Lastly I express my thanks to my publisher Kalpaz Publications.

Pralay Kant

The Proper Study of Mankind is Man

Alexander Pope

1

Introduction

When one thinks of Wordsworth's poetry it is his attitude towards Nature that immediately comes to one's mind. But Wordsworth has also written poems about mankind that are of even more interest. Humanity and Nature are in fact not separate in Wordsworth's poetry. His finest poetry is about people first and then about Nature. As he notes in "Tintern Abbey":

> ....For I have learned
>
> To look on nature, not as in the hour
>
> Of thoughtless youth, but hearing oftentimes
>
> The still sad music of humanity... (88-91)

Wordsworth writes in the "Preface" to the Lyrical Ballads (hereinafter, LB) of 1800 that his primary objective "in these poems was to choose incidents and situations from common life, and to relate or describe them, throughout, as far as was possible in a selection of language really used by men" (76-79). S.T. Coleridge, too, notes in the Chapter XIV of the Biographia Literaria :

The thought suggested itself (to which of us I don't recollect) that a series of poems might be composed of two sorts, in the one, the persons and characters were to be, in part at least supernatural.... [that is, in Coleridge's poems. For the second class, which comprised Wordsworth's poems] objects were to be chosen from ordinary life; the character and incidents were to be such as will be found in every village." (5)

This is one reason why Wordsworth has written not only in the LB but also elsewhere about persons belonging to the proletariat: that they are exemplars of common humanity. It is because of this that he is often described as a humanist, for one of the characteristics of humanism is its belief in "a universal and given human nature" (Gandhi 27). But how far this label of humanist is in fact really appropriate to Wordsworth's major poetry is what has been examined in this book. This chapter sketches a very brief history of the Western humanism tracing its origins in the ancient Greece and its development till the present time. It also studies its impact upon English poetry up to the time of Wordsworth.

Humanism has been a distinctive note in the European thought in the last four centuries. It should not be confused, however, with humanitarianism; the latter is concerned with according to Modern Oxford English Dictionary, 'Human Welfare" (Swanell 517) but popularly it means sympathy and compassion, whereas humanism is a philosophical term, which has been explained in various ways. Indeed, as Leela Gandhi remarks: "Humanism is a highly contentious term. As Bernouer and Mohan point out, for example, 'Christianity, the critique of Christianity, science, anti-science, Marxism, existentialism, personalism, National Socialism, and Stalinism have each won the label 'humanism' for a time' "(27).

Thus there are many definitions of humanism. The Modern Oxford English Dictionary defines it as :

1. An outlook or system of thought concerned with human rather than with divine and super natural matters.

2. A belief or outlook emphasizing common human needs a seeking solely rational ways of solving human problems.

3. Often (humanism) literary culture esp. that of the renaissance humanists. (Sullivan 517).

The Wikipedia defines humanism as:

a broad category of active ethical philosophies that affirm the dignity and worth of all people, based on the ability to determine *right and wrong* by appeal to universal human qualities—particularly rationalism. Humanism is a component of a variety of more specific philosophical systems, and is also incorporated into some religious schools of thought.

Humanism entails a commitment to the search for truth and morality through human means in support of human interests. In focusing on the capacity for self-determination, humanism rejects transcendental justifications, such as a dependence on faith, the supernatural, or divinely revealed texts. Humanists endorse universal morality based on the commonality of human nature, suggesting that solutions to our social and cultural problems cannot be parochial. (http://en.wikipedia.org/wiki/Humanism)

M. H. Abrams writes :

In the sixteenth century the word "humanist" was coined to signify one who taught or worked in the "*studia humanitatis*", or Humanities — that is, grammar, rhetoric, history, poetry and moral philosophy, as distinguished from fields less concerned with the moral and imaginative aspects and activities of man, such as mathematics, natural philosophy and theology....In the nineteenth century, a new word, humanism, came to be applied to the view of man, the general values, and the educational ideas common to many Renaissance humanists, as well as to later writers in the same tradition.

Typically, Renaissance humanism assumed the dignity and central position of human beings in the universe; emphasized the importance in education of studying classical imaginative and philosophical literature, although with emphasis on its moral and practical rather than its aesthetic values; and insisted on the primacy, in ordering human life, of reason (considered the distinctively human faculty) as opposed to the instinctual appetites and the "animal" passions... In our time the term "humanist" often connotes those thinkers who base truth on human experience and reason and base values on human nature and culture, as distinct from those who regard religious revelation as the warrant for all truth and values. With few exceptions, however, Renaissance humanists were pious Christians who incorporated the concepts and ideals inherited from pagan antiquity into the frame of the Christian creed. The result was that they tended to emphasize the values achievable by human beings in this world, and to minimize the earlier Christian emphasis on the innate corruption of human being and on the ideals of asceticism and of withdrawal from this world in a preoccupation with the world hereafter... The rapid advance in the achievements and prestige of the natural sciences and technology after the Renaissance sharpened, in later heirs of the humanistic tradition, the need too defend the role of the humanities in a liberal education against the encroachments of the sciences and the practical arts. (116-17).

Gandhi, too, has this to say:

These varying humanisms are, however, unified in their belief that underlying the diversity of human experience it is possible, first, to discern a universal and given human nature, and secondly to find it revealed in the common language of rationality...[Both Renaissance and Enlightenment] humanisms assert that all human beings are, as it were, the measure of all things... (27-29)

philosopher G.T.W. Patrick relates humanism with pragmatism. He negates philosophy that is too theoretical, too far removed from:

practical concerns, too metaphysical and scholastic .... I want philosophy of life - of Real life. Pragmatism is distinctly a philosophy of life. Life is real and the real is life. Life is decidedly a human philosophy and has sometimes been called Humanism. (320)

The term humanism is said to have been coined in 1808 by a German educationist, F.J. Niethammer, to describe an educational programme that focused on human interests and values rather than on science and technology. But humanism as an educational and philosophical outlook on life based on a belief in the importance of the individual and in human (as opposed to religious) values goes much further back. It had its roots in ancient Greece, in particular in Plato, Zeno, Epicurus and Aristotle. Different as these thinkers were from each other, they laid the foundations of a humanism based on reason, which shaped the individual's life and character.

This outlook continued for centuries, and may be noted in the philosophical and educational ideas of, among, others, Cicero, Marcus Aurelius, Seneca and Epictetus in ancient Rome. The classical Greeks were interested in an education that would develop the latent qualities of the individual; this would mean studying not just vocational or theological courses but those which would encourage these "humane" qualities. As de Burgh puts it, "The theme of Greek thought and literature was humanity; man as he is amidst actual environment". (520)

Humanism as a philosophy may be ancient, but the phrase humanist became current in English only during the Renaissance. The word was derived from the term *umanista,* used for teachers of the *studia humanitatis* ("humanistic studies") of the late Middle Ages, which consisted of all the subjects in the liberal arts educational curriculum, the *artes liberalis*, so called because they centered on the skills and knowledge human beings needed to be truly free. This comprised all the subjects usually studied at that time apart from theology and natural science : the *trivium* of grammar (which included history and literature), logic and rhetoric, and the *quadrivium* of geometry, arithmetic, astronomy and music. This education was based on Latin authors and classical texts read in anthologies and translations rather than in the original versions. The Italian scholars Coluccio Salutati and Leonardo Bruni used the *studia humanitatis* as the basis of understanding and dealing with other people and leading a life of active service to state and society. As Gandhi notes, "the rise of the *umanista* in mid-sixteenth century Italy marks the process whereby a set of vested interests starts to attach itself to the promotion of the liberal arts." (45)

Thus the rediscovery and re-evaluation of the civilization of ancient Greece and Rome, which was the starting-point of both humanism and the Renaissance, became a kind of reaction to the excesses of medieval scholasticism. *Literoe humaniores* was the expression used to refer to classical literature and its contemporary imitations, to contrast it with the *Literoe sacroe* of scholasticism, which by the end of the fourteenth century had sometimes become merely a matter of quarrelling over minor points in theology and philosophy, such as the notorious controversy about how many angels could dance on the head of a pin. The early humanists, contemptuous of such quibbling, propounded instead a return to the original classics rather than the commentaries preferred by the scholastics, because they believed in the limitless potential of the human mind and the use of human knowledge for the advancement of the individual and society. For these humanists, literature was the core of education, because it offered the only form of knowledge that human beings needed; thus Bruni praised literature for its universality and thus for providing a complete education, necessary even outside the classroom.

The European Renaissance, not surprisingly, made itself felt first in Italy, after the Turks had taken over Constantinople, the capital of the eastern Roman empire, in 1453. The Greek scholars in Constantinople now took refuge in Italy. They brought with them the ancient manuscripts written by ancient Greek scholars, and scattered all over Europe, thus bringing back that knowledge in Europe of which it had been deprived for many centuries. This revival was not confined to learning but spread to different fields of human activities such as religion, painting, commerce, architecture and navigation. In David Daiches' words :

Humanism had many aspects: The scholarly, concerned with the recovery or reconstitution of accurate texts of the classics; the stylistic, concerned with classical rhetoric and literary criticism and their application to an improved vernacular literature; the ethical, concerned with the highest ideals of Greek and Roman thought (which could be combined with or modified by Christian teaching); and what might be called the positively secular, the replacement of a theocentric universe by one based on man and his potentialities, the acceptance of human life and human values as of permanent significance in ordered and controlled by a sense of proportion, interpreted in the light of the best thought of antiquity, and enriched and illuminated by the arts. (146)

In England, humanism started later than the rest of Europe. Some Englishmen such as Thomas Linacres and William Grocyn had gone to the Italian ports of Florence, Padua, Rome and Venice in search of ancient texts, and on their return had established a school at Oxford. Atkins writes, "The early Italian humanists who guided the development of humanistic thinking in England were Laurentius Valla and Politian; but they also got valuable assistance from Vittorino da Feltre, Guarino da Verona, and Leonardo Bruni, besides Pico della Mirandola, Savonarola and Volla". (60). John Colet applied the critical methods developed in Italy to the study of the Bible, and was thus a Christian humanist, that is, one who was a pious Christian but who nevertheless stressed the importance of the values that could be achieved in this world rather than concentrating on what earlier thinkers had done, that is, on man's corruptibility after the fall, on the importance of asceticism and on a preoccupation with other-worldly things.

Desiderius Erasmus (1469-1536) of the Netherlands was the most influential of the Christian humanists. In his *Colloquies* and *Praise of Folly* (1500), Erasmus satirized the corruptions of his contemporaries, especially the clergy, which he contrasted with the teachings of the Bible, early Christianity, and the best of pagan thinkers. In his *Adages* (1500), he even suggested that Christian teachings were consistent with classical thought and pagan wisdom. Erasmus devoted most of his energy and learning in establishing sound editions of the sources of the Christian tradition, such as his Greek New Testament (1516) and translations of the Greek and Latin written by Fathers of the Church. Erasmus' friend Sir Thomas More (1478-1535) wrote a humanist critique of society, Utopia (1516), which attacked the corruptions of power, wealth, and social status. By the middle of the sixteenth century humanism had won wide acceptance as an educational system, in which reasoning was a tool of enquiry.

The revival of classical learning brought in its wake a new interest in the world of earthly existence for its own sake, which was unlike the medieval emphasis only on unworldliness and otherworldliness. The Renaissance is commonly described as man's discovery of himself and his world; accordingly, it encompassed an attitude to life which valued earth above heaven, the search for virtu and success above the search for justice, the individual above institutions, and secular human values above purely Christian ones.

Now, beauty became more important than religious improvement, and there was a new way of approaching old themes. For example, while art portrayed the old religious subjects, the Virgin Mary was now seen as a woman and not just an embodiment of holiness. Similarly, pagan images, symbols and ideas merged with Christian ones, as in the writing of Sir Thomas Browne or John Milton. Because man's dignity was important, each person was regarded as autonomous and was encouraged to develop his own abilities, Thus, Renaissance humanists believed that pursuing secular ideals was not only an appropriate occupation but also a worthy one. Associated with this was a new devotion to Nature and its beauty.

David Daiches calls the French essayist Montaigne a typical representative of Renaissance humanism, but adds that England had no such single figure whose philosophy and vision was so characteristically humanist :

> secular-minded, but not antireligious; curious about and tolerant of human foibles and attitudes; continually fascinated by the problems posed both by his own psychological and physical self and by the external world. (146).

Nevertheless, the empiricist philosophers Bacon and Hobbes, like Locke, Berkeley and Hume after them, showed the directions in which English humanism moved. Sukanta Chaudhuri writes that for Francis Bacon (1561-1626), "the mind of man is greater than the totality of the works he contemplates (Advancement, I, i. 3); 'the just and lawful sovereignty over men's understanding, by force of truth rightly interpreted, is that which approacheth nearest to the similitude of the divine rule' (Advancement, I. viii. 3: Johnston, 57)" (70). For Bacon, moreover, "knowledge is declared to a law to the will itself, and thus act simultaneously as an intellectual and a moral good" (66-67). Thus the pursuit of knowledge implies spiritual as much as intellectual development.

According to Bacon the mind must be freed of what he calls the four "Idols", prejudices or "errors" : the idol of the tribe, which are errors inherent in human nature; the idols of the den, which are peculiar to the individual, the idols of the market, which are due to the fallacious use of language;

and, lastly, the idols of the theatre, which are false tenets of philosophy and perverted rules of demonstration. In order to rid the mind of these idols or prejudices science must begin with doubt. Bacon always relates man with the universe.

> Man is placed at the centre of an inexhaustible play of forces. He may command this by an effort and discipline that is basically moral in nature, though intellectual in its sphere of operation. Such effort demands that we reject nearly everything that a more expansive humanity holds precious. (Chaudhuri 72)

The empiricism of Bacon during the High Renaissance developed in due course into the secular humanism of Hobbes. For Thomas Hobbes (1588-1679), man is naturally amoral. Consequently, the state to him is a custodian of morality, and he recommends absolute monarchy as the best form of government. As in the Natural world, he explains, so in the world of mankind motion and antagonism are the original conditions. Self-aggrandizement is the motive of human actions. In order to protect themselves from one another, men constituted the State, without which "the life of man is solitary, poor, nasty, brutish and short" (qtd. in de Burgh 270). Hobbes' analysis and rationality were appreciated by the Augustans; as Mulgrave wrote in his "Essay on Poetry" :

> While in dark ignorance we lay, afraid
>
> Of fancies, ghosts, and every empty shade,
>
> Great Hobbes appear'd, and by plain reason's light
>
> Put such fantastic forms to shameful fight.
>
> (qtd in Legouis and Cazamian 39)

Like the scholastic philosophers, the Augustans were sure of a divine order behind all things, but their certainty was due not to scholastic logic but to scientific proof.

The progress of science reinforced the position of reason. This is evident particularly in the views of John Locke (1632-1704), who is a classic representative of both empiricism and Enlightenment humanism. Locke proposed to apply to psychology the inductive tests and methods of Bacon. For Locke knowledge has two sources; through the senses and through perceptions, which are the interplay of senses received by observation, implication and through reflection and memory. For him the mind is a *tabula rasa*, a clean sheet, upon which impinge sense-impressions, "until sensation begets memory and memory begets ideas. All of which seemed to lead to the starting conclusion that since only material things can affect our sense, we know nothing but matter, and must accept a materialistic philosophy. If sensations are the stuff of thought, the hasty argued, matter must be the material of mind". (Will Durant 256). Consequently, everywhere in Augustan writing there is a renewed interest in the processes of the human mind, from the essays in the "Spectator" to Pope's "Essay on Man".

What can we reason, but from what we know?

Of man, what see we but his station here,

From which to reason, or to which refer?

(18-20)

Clearly, then, the Enlightenment belief in reason made humanism more and more independent of religion, and sometimes it was associated with deism, unbelief and a secular outlook on life. The faith in the dignity of the human being at times became a part of anti- or non-religious views, exalting reason and science above all other-worldly ideas and superstitions, and regarded humanity and human progress as the supreme meaning of history.

In this connection the philosophical ideas of Berkley (1685-1753) are of some interest. Berkeley's works, remarks Bertrand Russell, "undertake to prove that there is no such thing as matter at all, and the world consists of nothing but minds and their ideas.... Berkeley shows that existence of matter is capable of being denied without absurdity and that if there are any things that exist independently of us they cannot be the immediate objects of our sensations". (4). Thus for Berkeley the only reality is the reality of the mind: "there is nothing real except minds and their ideas ... anything else is inconceivable, and what is inconceivable cannot exist." (5).

David Hume's (1711-1776) An Enquiry in Human Understanding (1711-1788) and Of Critical Discourses (1748) suggest the finite nature of human faculties. He is sceptical about human nature. Durant notes, "Hume said that when reason is against a man, he will soon turn against reason" (260). Another important characteristic of Hume's thought is his criticism of the concept of causality : "A is the cause of B, thus B is produced by A by some hidden power. Hume asserts that there is no proof that there is some hidden power as implied but is simply the output of a sequence of events." (Miller 258).

The empiricists, then, contributed considerably to the development of humanist philosophy, and marked a change in direction from Renaissance humanism. That is why scholars today usually distinguish between two kinds of humanism: Renaissance humanism, which evolved into the area of studies called the humanities, and Enlightenment humanism, which, in Gandhi's words, "identifies humanism with the theory of subjectivity and knowledge inaugurated by Bacon, Descartes and Locke, and scientifically substantiated by Galileo and Newton" (28). There may be many differences between the two, but both are anthropocentric, and categorically valorise the human subject. For both, humanism is concerned with "humanness", which in turn is closely related to questions of knowledge. There is a symbiotic, reciprocal relationship between what man is, and what he knows: "Renaissance humanism and its inheritors insist that man is made human by what he knows", while in Enlightenment humanism, "humanness" is "a function of the way in which he knows things." Thus, where Renaissance humanism is predominantly concerned with the role and function of pedagogy, the Enlightenment furnishes the modern understanding of the self and subjectivity. (Gandhi 28-29).

There were two humanist philosophers, Jean Jacques Rousseau and William Godwin, whose impact on Wordsworth was enormous. They were both in the tradition of Enlightenment humanism, but with a difference. A few remarks about them would be useful.

Jean Jacques Rousseau (1712-1778), famous for the clarion call "Return to Nature" (qutd. in Crompton and Rickett 293), emphasised the importance of the individual man. He believed that culture and civilization had degraded society, and that men should go back to the old ways of living. Rousseau argued "that nature is good, and civilization bad, that by Nature all men are equal, becoming unequal only by class-made institutions, and that law is an invention of the strong to chain and rule the weak." (qtd. in Durant 3). Unlike the usual humanist, therefore, he was against reason.

Durant summarises Rousseau's views in these words: "in the novel complexities and artificialities of urban life, reason is the better guide, but in the great crises of life, and in the great problems of conduct and belief, we trust to our feelings rather than to our diagrams. If reason is against religion, so much the worse for reason." (259). In fact, whenever philosophy becomes important, the moral health of the nation decays: "I venture to declare that a state of reflection is contrary to nature and that a thinking man (an intellectual, as we would now say) is a depraved animal. It would be better to abandon our over-rapid development of the intellect, and to aim rather at training the heart and the affections. Education does not make a man good; it only makes him clever — usually for mischief. Instinct and feeling are more trustworthy than reason." (qtd. in Durant 260). These are ideas that recur in Wordsworth's poetry.

Rousseau believed, like Spinoza, that political philosophy must grow out of a distinction between the natural and the moral order — that is, between existence before, and existence after, the formation of organized societies. "Men once lived in comparative isolation, without law or social organization, there were then, he says, no conceptions of right and wrong, justice or injustice, might and right were one" (qtd. in Durant 190). Rousseau thus modified the theory of social contract formulated by Locke. Willey writes:

> In Wordsworth's lifetime this humanism had taken a colouring from Rousseau, and the special nobility of man was therefore only to be looked for 'in huts where poor men lie'. The 'higher' grades of society, in which the culture of the Renaissance had been exclusively fostered, were now
>
> 'A light, a cruel, and vain world, cut off

From the nature inlets of just sentiment,

From lowly sympathy, and chastening truth.'

(the PL, ix, 349).

Willey further writes: The blend of these two closely-related beliefs resulted, with Wordsworth, in his typical celebration of figures like the Leech-Gatherer, Michael, or 'Nature's Lady': beings whose humanity is ennobled by close association with 'mute insensate things' (308-309).

William Godwin (1756-1836) also influenced Wordsworth. His Inquiry Concerning Political Justice, and its Influence on General Virtue and Happiness (1793), was an iconoclastic work. One great failing of Rousseau, according to Godwin, was his deism. He himself was an atheist, and held that ideas are not inborn but are series of impressions formed out of association and reflection. According to Godwin, it is wrong to believe in the moral freedom of man. For him man has no independent will; therefore, as he says, "if languages are truly philosophical, it would contain no such expressions as "I will exert myself ... I will do this" (qtd. in Legouis 261). Godwin further argues that reason cannot function because it is hampered by political and religious institutions. Therefore there should be no political, social and religious institutions. Whether or not Wordsworth had read Political Justice, he must have been aware of the book's content, because it was a very popular work among young intellectuals of the time, and in fact in the Prelude he refers to the impact of its radical philosophy upon him when he was young, a radicalism which he had by then renounced. Besides, the man who had helped Godwin in publishing it had also helped Wordsworth in publishing The Excursion (1814).

During the nineteenth century, humanism began to absorb the growing importance of physics and biology and of the social sciences, especially political economy and sociology. So by the end of the century, the old subjects taught in the humanistic disciplines were often replaced by the newer areas of interest. This led to a collapse of older notions of humanism, which was further weakened by Nietzsche's invocation of the will to power and his challenge to the belief in truth. The theories of Freud, too, added to the decay of traditional humanism, because it stressed the irrational forces and the role of the unconscious in explaining human personality. Nevertheless, as has been suggested earlier, the humanism of some of the eighteenth-century European thinkers did include an anti-rational element, which is what lies beneath much of the humanism of the Romantic period.

The rise of Naturalism further accelerated the decline of traditional humanism, which the horrors of the World Wars also added to. The humanistic belief in the dignity and nobility of man and in human progress no longer seemed a valid idea for many thinkers. But the new anti-humanism was not the only trend in Western thought. The French philosopher and writer Jean-Paul Sartre regarded his existential ideas as being humanist, and Martin Heidegger also stressed the importance of humanism in his "Letter on Humanism". Thus the philosophical ideas of humanism continued into the twentieth century, in the New Humanism of Irving Babbitt and Paul Elmer More and with the formation of humanist societies like the Humanistic Religious Association formed as far back as 1853 in London and the First Humanistic Society of New York in 1929, with intellectuals like Julian Huxley, Albert Einstein, Thomas Mann and John Dewey as its advisors. The American

Humanist Association was established in 1941; Isaac Asimov was a president of this organization, and at present the novelist Kurt Vonnegut presides over it. In 1933 Raymond B. Bragg and others drafted a Humanist Manifesto, which was signed by thirty-four intellectuals, and which declared that:

> humanism will: (a) affirm life rather than deny it; (b) seek to elicit the possibilities of life, not flee from them; and (c) endeavor [sic] to establish the conditions of a satisfactory life for all, not merely for the few. By this positive morale and intention humanism will be guided, and from this perspective and alignment the techniques and efforts of humanism will flow.
>
> ...Though we consider the religious forms and ideas of our fathers no longer adequate, the quest for the good life is still the central task for mankind. Man is at last becoming aware that he alone is responsible for the realization of the world of his dreams, that he has within himself the power for its achievement. He must set intelligence and will to the task. (http://www.americanhumanist.org/about/manifesto1.html)

This was followed forty years later by the Humanist Manifesto II, published in the September/October 1973 issue of The Humanist magazine by the American Humanist Association, and was intended to update the previous one, which was facing the challenges of new times, especially after World War II. Accepting the fact that there were many kinds of humanism and numerous obstacles in the way of establishing a "humane" world order, this Manifesto reiterated the humanist commitment to the possibilities of human progress and to human values: "commitment to all humankind is the highest commitment of which we are capable; it transcends the narrow allegiances of church, state, party, class, or race in moving toward a wider vision of human potentiality. What more daring a goal for humankind than for each person to become, an ideal as well as practice, a citizen of a world community." (http://www.jcn.com/manifestos.html)

The Humanist Manifesto III of 2003, also called "Humanism and its Aspirations", was a successor to the first manifesto. It describes humanism as "a progressive philosophy of life that, without supernaturalism, affirms our ability and responsibility to lead ethical lives of personal fulfillment that aspire to the greater good of humanity", and adds: "The life stance of Humanism — guided by reason, inspired by compassion, and informed by experience — encourages us to live life well and fully." Behind it are the beliefs that "Humans are an integral part of Nature, the result of unguided evolutionary change"; that "Ethical values are derived from human need and interest as tested by experience"; that "life's fulfillment [sic] emerges from individual participation in the service of humane ideals", and, above all, that "The responsibility for our lives and the kind of world in which we live is ours and ours alone." "Humanism and Its Aspiration" (The New Humanist). 2003<(http://www.americanhumanist.org/3HumandIts Aspirations.htm).

Works cited

"Humanism and Its Aspiration" The New Humanist. 2003 <http://en.wikipedia.org/wiki/Humanism>

Abrams, M.H. A Glossary of Literary Terms. Bangalore: Eastern India Press, 2003.

Atkins, J.W.H. Literary Criticism : Renaissance. London: Methuen and Co., 1957.

Bragg, Raymond, "Humanist Manifesto-I". The Humanist. May-Jun, 1933 <http://en.wikipedia.org/wiki/Humanism>

Burgh, W.G. De. Legacy of the Ancient World, *Vol 2.* Hermondsworth: Pelican Books Ltd., 1953.

Chaudhari, Sukanta. Infirm Glory. London: Oxford University Press, 1981.

Coleridge, S.T. Biographia Literaria. Ed. J. Shawcross. London: Oxford University Press, 1962.

Crompton, A.C. Rickett. History of English Literature. New Delhi: Universal Press, 1980.

Daiches, David. From the begnings to the sixtenth century, *Vol 1*. New Delhi: Allied Publications, 1960.

Durant, Will. History of Philosophy. New York: Pocket Books Ltd., 1979.

Gandhi, Leela. Post-Colonial Theory. New Delhi: Oxford University Press, 1996.

Hope, Marjorie and Nicholson. A Reader's Guide to John Milton. London: James and Hudson, 1964.

Kurtz, Paul. "Humanist Manifesto-II" The New Humanist. Sep.-Oct., 1973 <http://en.wikipedia.org/wiki/Humanism>

Legouis, Emile and Louis Cazamian. History of English Literature. Trans. Helen Irvine. New Delhi : The Macmillan Ltd., 1987.

Legouis, Emile. The Early Life of Wordsworth : The Prelude, a Critical Study. New York: P. Dutton & Company, 1932.

Miller, Leo. F. History of Philosophy. New Delhi: Discovery Publishing House, 2002.

O'Neill, Judth, ed. "The Economic Determination of Jane Austen". By Leonar Woolf. Critics on Jane Austen. New Delhi : Universal Book Stall, 1992.

Patrick, G.T.W. Introduction to Philosophy. New Delhi: Surjeet Publications, 1980.

Russell, Bertrand. The Principles of Philosophy. Bombay: Oxford University Press, 1986.

Swannell, Julia, ed. The Modern Oxford English Dictionary. London: Oxford University Press, 1992.

Hutchinson, Thomas, ed. Poetical works of Wordsworth. London: Oxford University Press, 1953.

2

Humanism in English Poetry: From Renaissance to Romantics

From the brief account in the previous chapter it should be obvious that humanism has been a major influence upon English poetry, even before the Renaissance. In the medieval age William Langland and Geoffrey Chaucer may be seen to display the humanistic spirit much before the advent of humanism in England. But even before them there were the folk songs and minstrels of the mid-thirteenth century, which had started to satirize the landlords and the clergy. Thus "The Song of the Husbandsman" complains of the burden of taxes, the oppression of the bailiff and the wood ward, and even about the tyrannous King. Langland's allegorical poem "Piers Plowman" depicts the pitiable condition of the poor farmers during the reign of Kings Edward III and Richard II, even though its main thrust is to show the true path to heaven, and how it is the poor plowman rather than the priest who can lead the people there. Similar poems that focus on ordinary people and their ordinary lives are, for example, John Lydman's "London Lickpenny", and John Skelton's "The Rowge of Court", "The Boke of Colin Clout" and "Why Comeye to Cult". Gower, too reflects the conditions of the times in his poems. Geoffrey Chaucer (1342-1400), too, may be seen as a humanist. He also depicts the corruption in the church and the hypocrisy of medieval society, especially in his Canterbury Tales. The characters as presented in the "Prologue" show people as they are, not as they should be.

The first notable and clearly humanistic poet in English poetry is Edmund Spenser (1552-1599), who in his Faierie Queene depicts the virtues praised by the Renaissance humanism, such as chivalry, valour and honesty.
Chaudhari sums up his humanistic qualities when he writes:

Spenser uses humanity bodying forth order, beauty, love, human love, human chivalry, and ordered earthly society lose their stigma of sin and moral inadequacy and become lofty spiritual goals. His 'this-worldly' approach makes for a strikingly new treatment of traditional themes and images. (92)

The Renaissance humanist Philip Sidney (154-1686) praises poetry as the highest achievement of the human spirit. Choudhari writes, "This is no naive rhetoric on the excellence of poetry but a balanced piece of humanist optimism, utilizing mans imperfect nature to consolidate his assault on perfection" (54).

But humanism in the Renaissance is most obvious in the drama, of which Christopher Marlowe's (1565-93) Tragic Historie of Doctor Faustus is a prime example. The play reveals many of the characteristics of Renaissance humanism, in particular its intellectual and sensual curiosity, its hunger for power, knowledge and beauty. The play's protagonist Dr. Faustus craves for more and more knowledge and power, for which he sells his soul to Mephistopheles. Like many other men of his time, he devotes himself to the study both of science and literature. His long, intimate acquaintance with the Ancients has stamped his thought and language much more than his familiarity with law or theology. As a result of his study of Greek and Latin authors, he has assimilated their views on the destiny of man, and so this word 'damnation' does not terrify him. The conflict between the world of human needs and desires and the demands of religion — the fundamental conflict in Renaissance humanism — is never more clearly shown as in this play.

Not surprisingly, it is in Shakespeare's (1564-1616) plays that humanism in most evident in Renaissance drama. Hamlet, for example, is concerned not with man's religious beliefs but with the existential problems of everyday life. Indeed, Hamlet fails to take revenge because, as Chaudhari suggests, he is " unfit to express his humanity" (Chaudhari 145).

Hamlet also muses about man in the last soliloquy:

What is a man,

If his chief good and market of his time

Be but to sleep and feed? A beast, no more!

Sure he that made us with such large discourse,

(IV.iv. 33-36)

In King Lear the perception of human misery, of the protagonist is accompanied by the urge for action:

Take physic, pomp;

Expose thyself to fell what wretches feel,

That thou mayst shake the superflux to them,

And show the heavens more just. (III, iv, 33-6)

In Macbeth, notes Chaudhari, "from the outset, the fullness of Macbeth's humanity agitates him between an impossible range of contraries: honour and ambition, moral horror and irresistible temptation" (178). In the pursuit of his ambition, his virtu, he declares, "I dare do all that may become a man, etc.," (178), and when he decides to murder Duncan he detaches himself from mankind and its values:

Cancel and tear to pieces that great bond

Which keeps me pale.

(Macbeth, III, ii, 49-50)

In the Tempest, Shakespeare's one of the last plays, Miranda's comments in Act I Scene ii when she sees the other human being, Ferdinand, for the first time, are often referred to when speaking of the dramatist's humanism. Furthermore, the play today is seen as an allegory of colonialism through which the humanistic implications become apparent. Prospero is the symbol of the colonisers and the island he settles in is a colony over which he rules, with its inhabitants such as Caliban and Ariel, both of whom in their different ways hungry to be free. No wonder, then, that Caliban rejects the colonial subterfuge that Prospero and Miranda adopt to subjugate him when he tells them what he feels about their gift of language: "You taught me language; and my profit on't/Is, I know how to curse."(I.ii.365-6).

After Spenser the Renaissance poet who was most clearly a humanist is John Milton (1608-1674), who has been described by both Abrams and Douglas Bush as "Christian humanist". Most humanists today are secular, often agnostic thinkers, but Renaissance humanists were practising Christians, who incorporated the concepts and ideals of the classical world into their Christian beliefs. Accordingly, instead of concentrating on Original Sin, man's corruptibility, and the next world, they examined what human beings could achieve in this one, and their themes centered on human interests and moral concern rather than religion. Human dignity, the value of a life of action, and the belief in free will marked Renaissance humanism, and forms the basis of Milton's focus on human issues and problems in particular. This may be seen marked in everything he wrote, from his sonnets about liberty (for example, "On the Late Massacre in Piedmont", or the sonnet on the prisoners of Chillon) to Paradise Lost, Samson Agonistes and Paradise Regained. In fact, Harold Skulsky's recent book on Paradise Lost, Milton and the Death of Man, sees this long poem as a case of "Humanism on Trial" (the phrase is part of the subtitle of the book, Humanism on Trial in the Paradise Lost). In Paradise Lost Satan constantly struggles to free himself from the clutches of the God, a theme that is similar to Shelley's great lyrical drama Prometheus Unbound. Indeed, Milton has been said to be, in Blake's famous words, "on the devil's party whether he knew it or not; Satan is the hero of the Paradise Lost" (qtd. in Hope and Nicolson, 186). Milton's Satan declares, in humanistic tradition, that "It is better to rule in Hell, than to serve in Heaven" (Book I, 263), and that, "The mind is its own place, and it itself/Can make a Heaven of Hell, a Hell of Heaven". (254-55)

That is why Bush says: "Milton was an ardent, liberal humanist who rebel against scholastic" (20).

John Donne (1571/72-1631), the leading Metaphysical poet of the Sixteenth Century represents humanism of the philosophical kind and his love poetry is obviously humanistic. Donne was influenced by the by the new knowledge which was revolutionizing all the fields of human activities specially science. He writes in the poem "An Anatomy of the World".

And new philosophy calls all in doubt,

The element of fire is quite put out;

The sun is lost, and the earth, and no man's wit

Can well direct him where to look for it.

(qtd. in Trevor James 15)

Trevor James informs us that Donne was very curious and inquisitive about the New Knowledge and as has been seen earlier in the Chapter-I that curiosity and inquisitiveness were some of the leading characteristics of the Renaissance Humanism :

Donne's case the mix of medieval and new learning is particularly clear. His interest in astronomers such as Bruno, Kepler, Galileo and Copernicus, and the possible implications of their ideas is amply demonstrated in his writing. Similarly we know that he was familiar with Renaissance humanists such as Montaigne (15).

In the Augustan period the poetry of Alexander Pope in particular reveals the influence of humanism, as in his poem, "Essay on Man", which envisages great hope for man's abilities:

So man, who here seems principal alone,

Perhaps acts second to some sphere unknown.

(37-38)

But Pope was no exception in his revelation of the continuance of humanistic beliefs; throughout the Augustan period poets, dramatists, essayists and novelists disclosed in their work the humanistic ideas of the significance of the human being and of selfhood, and in reason and free will. There was, besides, another strain in eighteenth-century poetry that reveals humanism, and that is in the love of Nature and the expression of humanitarian feeling.

This is particularly evident in the poems of the precursors of the romanticism of the eighteenth century. Amongst the most prominent of them is James Thomson, with his sympathy with misery and oppression in all its forms, and in his descriptions of the cruelty and harshness with which people treated the inmates of asylums, prisons, orphanages and weak, convicted criminals. Professor Lovejoy has traced the presence of humanistic feeling in the influential teaching of the Cambridge Platonists, Richard Cumberland's Treatise of the Laws of Nature, and the recommendations of benevolence in the sermons of Tillotson, Barrow and Sherlock and to Shaftesbury's "Characteristics who had taken to heart his moral teaching" (77).

Thomas Gray's (1716-1771) humanism is seen in his compassionate treatment of poor villagers in his "Elegy Written in a Country Churchyard" about "The short and simple annals of the poor" (32). Indeed, he even appears to be republican when he thinks of villagers who may have died in fighting against their tyrannical landlord:

Some village Hampden, that with dauntless breast

The little tyrant of his fields withstood;

Some mute inglorious Milton here may rest,

Some Cromwell guiltless of his country's blood. (57-60)

Oliver Goldsmith (1730-1774) also displays humanist sensibilities in the poem "The Deserted Village"(1770) when he writes about the oppression of the poor farmers by the landlord. William Cowper's (1731-1800) poems, too show the influence of humanism. Thus "The Castaway"(1799) may be seen as the story of a man's struggle for survival. George Crabbe (1754-1832) also evinces humanistic qualities in his poems such as "The Village" and "The Borough" (1810). Crabbe in these poems raises certain social questions and wants answers. Thus in "The Borough" Peter Grimes alone is not responsible for the death of the two boys; the whole borough too is responsible. Through this story doubts are also raised about the functioning of the working houses of England.

Such Peter sought, and, when a lad was found,

The sum was dealt him, and the slave was bound. (65-66)

As Hatch writes:

Crabbe does not divide man into psychological, social, moral and religious aspects, but creates an aesthetic unity in which they are presented as ways of seeing man. In so doing, Crabbe comes close to achieving the impossible, writing social criticism which does not place all the onus for the trouble on 'society', but which reveals that the economic forces of society are themselves rooted in man's perception of himself. The social reformer generally deals with the social causes, the artist with the human. Only rarely are they combined successfully'. 'Peter Grimes' is an outstanding example of such a success. (196).

William Blake (1757-1827) also evinces humanism in such poems as "Black Boy", "Holy Thursday-II" and "The Tyger". In the "Black Boy" Blake goes against the prevailing Racism of Europe in his sympathetic portrayal of the black boy who is unhappy because of his colour and complaints about this to his mother:

My mother bore me in southern wild

and I am black, but oh! my soul is white

(1-2)

Even though the theme of the poem is religious: "Look on the rising sun: there God does live/And gives his light, and gives his heat away; (9-10), but considering the fact that the Apartheid (segregation of Negro) only ended in the early 1990's in the South Africa, it is very commendable on the part of Blake to write on anti racialism almost more than two hundred and fifty years ago.

Blake though is deeply religious poet but at times he goes against Christianity and to go against religion is one of the foremost qualities of humanism. In the "Tyger" he writes:

What immortal hand or eye,

Dare frame thy fearful symmetry?

(3-4)

Blake does not answer this question, may be in the poem, he thinks it to be unanswerable Prof. Kermode believes that: "immortal hand or eye belonged only to Man," who is terrified by a monster of his own creation. The orthodox Christian mythology cannot answer these questions as they are far beyond its grasp. Man as a creator can be much more Satanic than Satan himself.

(qtd. in Shrivastava, 73-74)

Robert Burns's (1759-96) poetry about common people, from village folk to murderers, is also humanistic, like "Tam O' Shanter".

It should be evident from the above, then, that there was a long tradition of humanistic poetry in English that prepared the ground for Wordsworth and the other Romantics. At this point it would be useful to mention a few details about Wordsworth's life and poetic career, to understand how humanism entered into his mental make-up.

Wordsworth's father, John, was an attorney at-law at Cockermouth in Cumberland; his mother was the daughter of a mercer at Penrith. The poet was the second of five children, and was born on the 7th April, 1770, the year that Chatterton died and Goldsmith's "The Deserted Village" was published. His parents died early and he was taken to his maternal grandparents, the Cooksons, and was brought up under the guardianship of his uncles. The Cooksons were not forthcoming people; they were harsh, and at times the orphans were subjected to reproach and insults. His childhood, therefore, was not a particularly happy one. The young boy turned to Nature as companion and solace, as is evident in both "Tintern Abbey" and The Prelude: "For nature then/...To me was all in all" ("Tintern Abbey", 72-72). His love of Nature, in fact, led him to love man; he titles the eighth Book of The Prelude "Retrospect. — Love of Nature Leading to Love of Man". At the age of eight he was sent to Hawkshead Grammar School (1778-1787). Many writers have found their school experiences unpleasant, such as Charles Dickens or the French writers Alfred de Vigny and Victor Hugo. Wordsworth, however, found his school life enjoyable and fruitful because as Legouis remarks, of "its freedom and natural life provided to its pupils" (31).

Dorothy, Wordsworth's sister, had a strong influence over him. After losing his mother at eight, Wordsworth had become strongly attached to his sister. When he became independent, brother and sister decided to remain together in a bond no force could sever. Wordsworth dedicated his first collection of poems, Descriptive Sketches, to her, which she had revised and even suggested certain corrections.

Wordsworth left Hawkshead at the age of seventeen and half and went to St John's College, Cambridge, where he stayed till 1791. Their father's employer, Sir James Lowther, who later became the Earl of Lonsdale, had coerced him to give him five thousand pounds, which, however, he refused to pay to the children after their father's death. The Wordsworth's were involved in a long legal suit to get their due, which they did after twenty long years, by that time they had risen to high positions in society: the eldest brother, Richard, became a barrister like his father, John became a professor at Cambridge, and the youngest, Christopher, became the captain of a ship. Dorothy did not marry and remained with the poet throughout her life. Wordsworth could not avail of this money when he needed it the most for his education and career. As a result of this prolonged legal battle the Wordsworths lived in a great penury and were dependent on their maternal relatives for their education and careers.

Wordsworth visited London for the first time in the autumn of 1788, and during his Long Vacations went to Penrith and on a walking tour through France and Switzerland in 1790. After graduating in 1791 he went abroad again to France. Notably, both trips were made in the thick of the French Revolution. In 1792 at Orleans he came in touch with a sergeant, Michel Beaupuy, of the 32nd Infantry, which was engaged in fighting the revolutionaries. Though the officer was fighting for the cause of the French monarchy he himself was in favour of the Republicans, and he and Wordsworth came close to each other. Beaupuy's religion was humanity, a love which was shared by Wordsworth. Beaupuy instilled in the poet the teachings of the French philosopher, Rousseau, and the English one, William Godwin, and thus became his revolutionary mentor. Wordsworth at first was not convinced by his Republican arguments, but the former demonstrated the poverty and the cruelty of the aristocrats through the harrowing tales of the ordinary French men women and their children. The turning point came when they were passing through a village that they saw a poor girl holding a cow with a string that Beaupuy exclaimed, "'T'is against that/ that we are fighting,' I with him believed/ That a benignant spirit was abroad." (The Prelude, ix, 560-562). It is then that Wordsworth became a staunch devotee of the Revolution. Legouis writes about this incident:

> Possibly this commonplace incident, with the phrase "I'is against that that we are fighting" which assuredly was uttered with the noble fire of passion did more than all the rest to complete Wordsworth's conversion. (212)

In fact, Wordsworth was on the point of offering himself as a leader of the Girondins (Hutchinson, "Chronological Table", xxiv). This sympathy for the republican movement was reinforced by his having fallen in love with Marie Anne Vallon, also called Annette by Wordsworth, the daughter of a revolutionary; his daughter Caroline by Vallon was born on December 15, 1792. However, he was recalled to England at the end of 1792, shortly after Caroline's birth.

Wordsworth returned to England in 1793 with his heart full of sympathy for the poor and the unfortunate, and while he went on visits to Bath, Bristol and Tintern Abbey, he also went to France again in October that year. He was shocked by England's declaration of war against France, but the French Revolution had turned into a gory event afterwards, and Wordsworth describes the effect of the Reign of Terror upon him in The Prelude Book X, In France, the men, who, for their desperate ends,/Had plucked up mercy by the roots were glad of this new enemy..... (331-333). But this did not move the poet away from his firm believe in the cause of the betterment of humanity, as seen, again, in the tenth Book of The Prelude, Then was the truth received in the my heart,/That, under heaviest sorrow earth can bring, (463-464). The French Revolution had in the end established a Republic, albeit over the blood of thousands of people, but Wordsworth continued to have hopes of improving the miserable conditions of the human lot. It had, after all, firmly planted the seeds of a just and egalitarian society for posterity and it proved to be a major inspiration for the successful revolutions of the twentieth century. Wordsworth remained profoundly influenced by its humanitarian ideals and there should not be no doubts that Rousseau and the French Revolution were the major impetus on the mind of the poet who wrote the humanistic poems of the Lyrical Ballads.

After coming back from France Wordsworth found that the English politicians such as Burke and Pitt were against

France and favoured the war with France. The Bishop of landoff Richard Watson who was earlier a supporter of France later became a reactionary and attacked France in his writings. Wordsworth wrote a letter to him attacking his views, the letter was never published. In this letter Wordsworth summarises his Republican views; he is against all kinds of religious institutions, private labour and private property, advocates laws that would improve the living conditions of the peasants and the workers, and wants to dispense with all kinds of titles that makes the English society the most unequal one in the world. He writes:

> ... Liberty is too often obliged to borrow the very arms of Despotism in order to overthrow him, and in order to reign in peace must establish herself by violence. She deplores such stern necessity, but the safety of the people, her supreme law, is her consolation. (qtd. in Legouis 228)

It will not be a misnomer to claim this letter of Wordsworth as a 'Communist Manifesto' of the Romantic Age. In a sense, Wordsworth's avowal to pick up arms to save liberty and peace makes him a Marxist much before Marxism was even thought of. It is note worthy that Leonard Woolf calls Jane Austen "Antithesis to capitalism." (qtd. in Judth O'Neill 52) for depicting economic inequalities.

After Dorothy the person who influenced Wordsworth the most was Samuel Taylor Coleridge (1775-1834), whom he met in 1795. Wordsworth himself said that "his intellect had owed an important debt to him, and that the influence of Coleridge had penetrated to his heart of heart" (qtd. in Legouis 222), and acknowledged Coleridge as the "most wonderful man he had ever known" (qtd. in Legouis 294). One of the greatest debts that Wordsworth owed to Coleridge was the latter's knowledge of philosophy, and particularly that of German Idealists such as Kant. This can be seen in such poems as "Tintern Abbey" and "The Immortality Ode". Coleridge was the first literary figure to recognise the poetic genius of Wordsworth. He described him as "the Milton of the age" (qtd. in Legouis 225). Their friendship continued until Coleridge died in 1834, although there was a quarrel in 1810 and a subsequent estrangement for some time.

Wordsworth married Mary Hutchinson in 1802 and continued to live at Dove Cottage, where he had settled since 1800. He moved to Allan Bank in 1809 and later to Rydal Mount and other places in the Lake District. Dorothy's mind gave way in 1835 and this was a great blow to the poet. Nevertheless, he continued his literary and intellectual activities. He was given a pension from the Civil List by the courtesy of Sir Robert Peel in 1842, and was made the Poet Laureate the following year. He died on April 2, 1850, and was buried in Grasmere.

In 1798 Wordsworth's most famous work Lyrical Ballads and other Poems was published, which he and Coleridge had planned together. In 1800 the second edition of the LB came out along with the Preface. Wordsworth wrote the drama Borders (1782), the only drama he wrote in his life. This is described by Legouis as "Godwinian". (30) In 1805 his second collection of poems was published. This was followed by The Excursion (1814) and, posthumously, The Prelude (1850). The following chapters examine the humanism that the major poems of Wordsworth evince.

Works Cited

Alisson, Alexander and Barrow, ed. The Norton Anthology of Poetry. New York: W.W. Norton Corp. Ltd., 1983.

Bush, Doughlas. John Milton. London: Weiden Field and Nicholson, 1964.

Couch, Arthur and Dover Wilson, ed. The Tempest. London: Cambridge University Press, 1965.

Ford, Boris. From Bacon to Johnson. London: Penguin Publications Ltd., 1960.

James, Trevor. The Metaphysical Poets. Harlow: Longman, 1988.

Judith, O'Neill. Critics on Austen. New Delhi: Universal Books Stall, 1982.

Knight, Wilson. Crown of Life. London: Oxford University Press, 1992.

Marlowe, Christopher. Doctor Faustus. Madras: The Macmillan Ltd., 1970.

Milton, John. Paradise Lost I & II. Ed. E.T. Prince. London: Oxford University Press, 1976.

Rickett, Edith and Olson, Clair. The World of Chaucer. New York: Columbia University Press, 1950.

Robinson, E.W., ed. Chaucer : A Prologue to the Canterburry *Tales.* London: Oxford University Press, 1983.

Shakespeare, W. Hamlet. Ed. A.W. Verity. London: Cambridge University Press, 1966.

Shakespeare, W. King Lear. Ed. A.W. Verity. London: Cambridge University Press, 1966.

Shakespeare, W. Macbeth. Ed. J.R. Brown. London: Edward Arnold (Publishers) Ltd., 1967.

Shakespeare, W. The Tempest. Ed. Arthur Couch and Dover Wilson London: Cambridge University Press, 1965.

Edt. Shrivastava, S.B. An Anthology of English Literature. Bhopal: Madhya Pradesh Hindi Granth Academy, 2003.

Tillyard, E.M.W. Studies In Milton. London: Chatau and Windmus, 1960.

Watson, J.B., ed. Pre Romanticism of the Eighteenth Century. London: Mac Millian Ltd., 1989.

Watson, J.R., ed. "Crabbe and Social Questions". By K.B. Hatch. Pre Romanticism of the Eighteenth Century. London: The Macmillan Ltd., 1989, 230.

3

Humanism in the Lyrical Ballads -1798

As historians of English literature have often noted, with the anonymous publication of the Lyrical Ballads and Other Poems (hereinafter LB) on 15th September 1798 by Wordsworth and Coleridge, a new era began in the history of English literature: it heralded the revival of Romanticism in the eighteenth century. There were twenty-three poems in the first edition of the LB; nineteen poems were contributed by Wordsworth, and just four by Coleridge: "The Dungeon", 'The Foster-Mother's Tale", "The Nightingale, a Conversational Poem ", and the first poem of the collection, the "Rime of the Ancyent Marinere".

In the previous chapter Coleridge's account of the design of the LB was referred to, in which he stated that in Wordsworth's poems "objects were to be chosen from ordinary life; the characters and incidents were to be such as will be found in every village." Mention had also been made of Wordsworth's 1800 Preface to the LB, which declared his choice of subject for his poems, and offered reasons for his decision :

> Humble and rustic life was generally chosen because in that condition the essential passions of the heart find a better soil in which they can attain their maturity, are less under restraint, and speak a plainer and more emphatic language; because in that condition of life our elementary feelings co-exist in a state of greater simplicity, and consequently, may be more accurately contemplated, and more forcibly communicated; because the manners of rural life germinate from those elementary feelings, and from the necessary character and rural occupations, are more easily comprehended, and are more durable and lastly, because in that condition the passions of men are incorporated with the beautiful and permanent forms of nature". (the Preface to LB, 96-98)

It is these ideas that made Michael H. Friedman call Wordsworth "a Tory humanist" in the title of his book The Making of a Tory Humanist: William Wordsworth and the Idea of Community. It is for this reason, too, that Helen Darbyshire comments on Wordsworth's decision:

> The poems of the 1798 volume represent Wordsworth's voyage into that elemental world of human suffering that exists on the fringes of society, and he enters that world in a spirit of selfless compassion that embraces the outcast, the rejected, the desolate, and the deranged. (Qtd. in Jones and Tydeman 16).

Robert Mayo has pointed out that Wordsworth's choice of subject was not unprecedented:

> Considered strictly in terms of subject and sentiments, most of the poems in the 1798 edition, it is clear, would not

seem anomalous or outlandish to contemporary readers. It is precisely in the direction of 'nature', 'simplicity, and sentimental humanitarianism that a minority of popular contemporary poets had already moved". (qtd. in Jones and Tydeman 97).

Clearly, it is Wordsworth's humanitarian instincts that lie behind his poems in the LB, and certainly all of them may be called "humanist" from this point of view. But, as has been suggested earlier, there is more to Wordsworth's humanism than simple humanitarianism.

It may be noted in this connection that Wordsworth's choice of diction for the poems in the LB may also be put down to the humanist influence. He has chosen to write in a "selection of language really used by men" from "humble and rustic life" (Preface to the LB, 86):

Because such men hourly communicate with the best objects from which the best part of language is originally derived; and because, from their rank in society and the sameness and narrow circle of their inter- course, being less under the influence of social vanity, they convey their feelings and notions in simple and unelaborated expressions. Accordingly, such a language, arising out of repeated experience and regular feelings, in a more permanent, and a far more philosophical language, than that which is frequently substituted for it by Poets. (the Preface to the LB, 101-110).

This is not only "human-centred" language, but humanist in another sense as well. James Downey's talk on "A Humanist Meets his Waterloo" makes this point clear:

The study of language is in the first instance, and above all, a quest for what is essentially human, for the defining feature of our being, for that which sets us most clearly apart from the rest of animal nature. To study language, therefore, is to explore the complexity and diversity of our minds and our emotions. It is to address a series of technical and philosophical questions which go to the heart of our individual and collective identities. To what extent does the language we speak and write condition perception and shape experience? Under what social and political conditions does language become debased, and what are the consequences of the debasement? A humanist's interest in language goes beyond the attempt to understand how it works, to a concern for the way in which it is used. (http:// www. communications.uwaterloo.ca).

Some comment about the use of the term ballad in the title of the anthology is needed at this point. One of the most striking features of pre-Romantic poetry was its interest in the folk or popular ballad, renewed by the publication of Bishop Percy's Reliques of Ancient English Poetry in 1765, and reinforced by the interest in the "folk" literature of ancient and medieval Britain that encouraged the composition of a large number of "literary" ballads Jacobus says: "Percy's anthology and the work of a German poet Gottfried Burger were the immediate literary influences behind Wordsworth's use of the term ballad for these poems" (233), but, as his "Yarrow" poems make it clear, they were not the only sources of inspiration. It is obvious that Wordsworth's poems in this volume are not ballads from the point of view of form, for they do not use the ballad metre, nor the characteristic refrain and mnemonic song-like style. Nevertheless, because they are about ordinary rustics and are simply related by an objective narrator, depict foreshortened action, and are frequently in dialogue form, Wordsworth's "lyrical ballads" are indeed ballads, even if their action moves not on the physical or material plane but on the emotional one. Indeed, as Jacobus points out, Wordsworth experiments with the ballad "produced some of his most provocative redefinitions" of the term ballad (232):

> The ballad-reader's expectation are aroused, disappointed — and redirected towards what were for Wordsworth more significant aspects of human experience, His achievement is to adapt the ballad to portraying those states and feelings least susceptible to narrative presentation. At the same time, he forces us to reassess the importance of the everyday. (233)

Jacobus goes on to point out:

> These ballads show Wordsworth challenging the genre he has adopted — insisting first on writing with a definite 'purpose', then on questioning the very basis of narrative convention, and finally subverting it altogether. The result is a genre capable not simply of expressing Wordsworth's vision, but of modifying and extending the reader's; offered 'Such stories as silent thought can bring', we are shown how to 'find A tale in everything'. The ballads of 1798 are not only technically exhilarating in their own right, but among Wordsworth's most effective statements about the aims and functions of his poetry. (Jacobus 234).

This, again, is what helps to make Wordsworth's "ballads" humanist.

Wordsworth was also influenced by Hannah More's religious tracts, of which some of the most popular were "The Roguish Miller", "Nothing got by cheating" (1795), and "Tragedy; showing how a servant maid first robbed her master, and was afterwards struck dead for telling a lie:: A True Story" (1796). But there is a difference between Hannah More's writings and Wordsworth's ballads : where

More wished to "edify the semi-literate, Wordsworth was asking his literate readers to think about their own code". (Jacobus, 239). A brief study of the individual poems will make this point clear.

The ballad "Goody Blake and Harry Gill" may be seen as humanist in the sense of revealing Wordsworth's humanitarianism. It also reveals the influence of philosophical humanism. The poem was influenced by an episode from Darwin's Zoonomia ; or, the Laws of Organic Life (1794-6), and Wordsworth calls it "A True Story". The poem begins by wondering why the young and well-to-do drover Harry Gill is always so cold, his teeth chattering continuously, summer or winter, night or noon, even though he is so warmly clad. The third stanza begins to explain why, with a contrast between the young, healthy and strong Harry and the old, poverty-stricken Goody Blake, who lives alone on an exposed and cold hillside. The old woman spins to keep her body and soul together. Winter makes her life even more difficult, but sometimes she welcomes the chilly wind because it leaves "scattered many a lusty splinter" (51), which keep her warm for three days. But when her stock of splinters gets depleted she is left with no respectable way of keeping herself warm, but to steal sticks from the hedge of Harry Gill's field. One day Harry catches her red-handed when she is pulling up sticks from the hedge. He holds her fast and "shakes" her so "fiercely" (91) that her bundle of sticks falls from her lap. She now turns to God who is "the judge of all" (96) and curses Harry :

> God ! who art never out of hearing,
>
> O may he never more be warm. (99-100)

After this Harry finds he can never keep himself warm, no matter how many blankets and warm clothes he wears.

As Jacobus points out, Goody Blake's appeal 'To God that is the judge of all" challenges the property values which for Harry had transcended humanity. Thus the poem, shows "the power of imagination to enforce humane values" (233), and also how "Wordsworth has subverted a genre which his contemporaries were accustomed to think of as educating the poor not only in virtue, but in acceptance of the status quo" (237). Goody Blake does not accept the fact that she is stealing and instead curses the person from whom she has stolen; her curse, moreover, comes true, though it is she who is in the wrong, legally speaking. Her defiance is the voice of human protest against a logic and reasoning that do not take human considerations into account. It thus goes against the eighteenth century belief in the importance of maintaining established social norms and becomes, instead, an expression of humanist ideas. Thus one can see how effectively Wordsworth has used all the features of the ballad form such as simple language, an objective narrator and the dialogue form to narrate the story of Harry Gill and Goody Blake which facilitates not only this poem but the poems to follow.

The "Idiot Boy" and "The Thorn" are among Wordsworth's favourite poems in the LB. Writing to his friend John Wilson in June 1802, Wordsworth described how much pleasure he derived while composing and reading "The Idiot Boy" :

I have often applied to idiots, in my own mind, that sublime expression of Scripture that Their Life is Hidden with God. They are worshipped, probably from a feeling of this sort, in several parts of the East... I have, indeed, often looked upon the conduct of parents, in the lower ranks of society, toward idiots as a great triumph of the human heart.

It is there that we see the strength, disinterestedness, and grandeur of love; nor have I ever been able to contemplate an object that calls out so many excellent and virtuous sentiments without finding it hallowed thereby, and having something in one which bears down before it like a deluge every feeble sensation of disgust and aversion." (qtd. in Jones and Tydeman 212).

The ballad is about a mentally retarded ("idiot") boy, Johnny, who is sent on horseback by his mother, Betty Foy, to bring a doctor from the town to attend to their terribly sick old neighbour, Susan Gale, as there is no-one else who can help them. She urges him to come back to her immediately, and Johnny seems to understand. But once he mounts the pony, he is entranced by the freedom and the joy of movement :

> But when the Pony moved his legs,
>
> Oh! then for the poor Idiot Boy!
>
> For joy he cannot hold the bridle,
>
> For joy his head and heels are idle,
>
> He's idle all for very joy. (72-76)

while Betty's heart is filled with pride, and happiness and hopes that her "idiot boy" is able to do something useful and enjoy doing it as well :

> And while the Mother, at the door,
>
> Stands fixed, her face with joy o'erflows,
>
> Proud of herself, and proud of him. (87-89)

But the doctor does not come, nor does Johnny return. The mother is distracted with worry about her son, and in the end leaves her ailing friend alone late in the night to search for him. When she reaches the doctor's house he tells her Johnny has not been there. She is so anxious that she forgets to ask the doctor to see Susan, but goes in search for Johnny. She runs into the woods, wondering whether he is dead, alive, and finally, near a waterfall, she finds the pony and then Johnny himself laughing happily. Susan too, is so worried about the missing boy that her body recovers, "As if by magic cured'. (426), and she goes looking for him herself as well. There is rejoicing because Johnny has been restored to them. But when he is asked later what had happened, all that he can answer is:

The cocks did crow to-whoo, to-whoo,

And the sun did shine so cold! (450-451)

Wordsworth's sympathy with the "idiot" is in stark contrast to Godwin's ideas about the mentally challenged. The latter held that they have no place in society because they do not have the power of reason, and can make no rational or useful contribution to society. Wordsworth, however, shows that Johnny is not useless. He is the centre of his mother's existence whom she loves dearly. Not only does Betty hope that Johnny will be able to bring the doctor, the joy that she feels when he is found, a joy that her friend, too, shares, reveals the real contribution he makes to society, through the happiness he can give people.

The traditional ballad is usually about acts of physical courage and often involves the supernatural. In this poem, however, as Jacobus suggests, the tradition of supernatural adventure is subverted, and instead, what is emphasized are "the feelings and experiences which irradiate the everyday" (233). This, again, is an example of the impact of the humanism of Rousseau and others like him. Throughout the poem the world of human confusion and distraction is contrasted with the silent unity of a permanent, enduring world of landscape. This helps to extend the boundaries of human sympathy, to refine the reader's sensibilities which is a part of the task of humanism.

The pride, hopes, and fears of the mother are narrated almost impersonally, in keeping with the ballad tradition, so that the distinction between the physical and the psychological dissolves; the world of feeling becomes one with the outer world of the senses and the landscape. This is a world that is inarticulate, the world of the boy who cannot say much more than "burr", of a mother's love that takes her from pride to anxiety to desperation and finally to joy, although she can hardly express these emotions in rational, logical terms.

"The Thorn" also reveals both humanitarianism and the influence of eighteenth century humanism. The entire poem is in quotation marks, suggesting that it is a dialogue between a story-teller who is close to the incident described, and a listener whose questions propel the narrative forward. The poem begins with a description of an old "Thorn", "a mass of knotted joints,/A wretched thing forlorn" (8-9). The bush is overgrown with lichen and mass, and beside it is a little pool of water and a "mound, which is a fresh and lovely sight" (35), which looks like an infant's grave. The place is deserted and frightening. It is said that a woman in a scarlet cloak comes there regularly to cry "Oh misery! oh misery!". (65).

The narrator explains that this woman is Martha Ray, whose beloved, Stephen Hill, on their wedding day itself had deserted her and married somebody else. Poor Martha had turned mad with grief. She was pregnant at that time, and what happened to that child she was expecting nobody knows. All that is certain is that every day Martha comes up to the Thorn and cries “Oh misery ! oh misery !”, even in “mist and rain, and storm and rain” (177). People says that she must have killed her new born-baby on the Thorn-tree or drowned it in the pool nearby, or buried it under the mound, but nobody knows for sure. It is believed that the moss is “spotted red” (210) and that the pool reflects a baby's face. When an attempt was made to dig up the mound to discover the body, says the narrator, so that Martha could be punished for murdering her child:

> ... instantly the hill of moss,
>
> Before their eyes began to stir!
>
> And, for full fifty yards around.
>
> The grass it shook upon the ground. (225-228)

The poem is thus the story of a possible crime, like many popular “murder ballads”, but instead of focusing on the crime, as the conventional murder-ballads did (and continued to do) it focuses on the woman's suffering, by narrating her story indirectly, through the voice of a sympathizer, whose attitude contrasts with those villagers who believe the woman must be punished. The story thus explores not what the woman had done but on her predicament, the misery of her emotional condition. In this connection Darbishire's comments are relevant:

Nature seems to sympathise with her love and suffering. She has covered with beautiful mosses the little mound where the child lies buried. This points to a more complete poetic truth. As we have seen, nature's sympathy also manifests itself in a more active way, at least to the old man's [the narrator's] imagination. And it is highly significant of his bias that the third supernatural event should prove more acceptable to him than the other two.... Martha Ray is rescued from the hostility of the villagers by the miraculous intervention of nature. (qtd. in Jones & Tydeman 231)

"The Convict" describes the condition of a convict who is condemned to die. He may be a criminal, but the poet's humanitarian instincts are aroused when he sees "That outcast of pity "(13) :

'Tis sorrow enough on that visage to gaze,

That body dismiss'd from his care;

Yet my fancy has pierced to his heart, and portrays

More terrible images there.

(17-20)

When the convict asks the narrator why he has come to meet him the latter replies that he has done so "as a brother thy sorrows to share"(49).

No matter how terrible his crime, so dreadful that "At thy name though compassion her nature resign/Though in virtue's proud mouth thy report be a stain" (49-50), the narrator would, if it were possible, to "Would plant thee where yet thou might'st blossom again" (52). "This is a reiteration of Wordsworth's attacks on the penal system and his known advocacy of transportation as an alternative to prison." (Haveley 20)

The poem “Lines Left upon a seat in a Yew-tree” was completed in 1795. The poem reveals Wordsworth’s humanitarianism as well as the influence of Renaissance humanism. The poem is about a young scholar who in his youth was interested in science but later was led by Nature to “lofty hopes” (14) about the world. He cherished these hopes and ideals, but the world ignored God’s “favoured being”. (16) The scholar was not prepared for neglect, and angrily he cut himself off from the world. He used to spend all his hours alone on that seat, “And with the food of pride sustained his Soul” (23), thinking only about his unproductive life and gazing at the beauty of Nature rather than other human beings. The narrator cautions the reader about pride, which is really nothing but “littleness” (52) :

True knowledge leads to love;

True dignity abides with him alone

Who, in the silent hour of inward thought,

Can still suspect, and still revere himself,

In lowliness of heart. (60-64)

The humanism in the poem is revealed in the rejection of pride and the reiteration about the importance of the community and the ties amongst people. Moreover, it is made clear that knowledge derived from books and self-love are always inferior to human relationships.

In the poem “Lines composed a Few Miles above Tintern Abbey” one can see both humanitarian and philosophical humanism. Both are evident when Wordsworth’s love of Nature leads to the love of man as has also been pointed out in a previous chapter. From a sensuous delight in Nature:

To me was all in all.-I cannot paint
What then I was. The sounding cataract
Haunted me like a passion: the tall rack,
The mountain, and the deep and gloomy wood,
Their colours and their form, were then to me
An appetite; a feeling and a love,
That had no need of a remoter charm,
By thought supplied, nor any interest
Unborrowed from the eye.-That time is past. (75-83)

Wordsworth turns to writing poetry about mankind. Thus the title of the eight book of the Prelude is "The love of Nature leading to Love of Man". Indeed, the very descriptions of Nature in "Tintern Abbey" include the human aspect, from the beginning of the poem with its depiction of the landscape in terms that emphasize human habitation, with its "plots of cottage-ground" (11), its orchards, household smoke coming out of the woods and even from a hermit's cave – thus linking a hermit, who has apparently renounced the world, to the everyday, "hedgerows"(15), and so on, to the way in which Nature can be a solace and a comfort to the individual hurt and disturbed by the rigours of contemporary urban life, represented by: "lonely rooms...towns and cities", a world of "rash judgments", full of the "sneers of selfish men" and hypocrisy (129-30). Moreover, Nature is dear to the poet because its memories can influence the human being to perform "acts/Of kindness and of love" (34-5). In fact, Nature is the :

The anchor of my purest thoughts, nurse and guide

The guide, the guardian of my heart, and soul

Of all my moral being. (109-11)

This again is an example of Enlightenment humanism, by its emphasis not on Nature but on what it means to humanity in day-to-day existence. The poem's account of Wordsworth's progress from an identification with the sensuous joys of Nature to an empathy with humanity is well known and has often been stressed; this has also been referred to the first chapter as well. The poem has undergone feminist, ecocritical, New Historicist and political readings, all of which should place it firmly in the humanistic tradition.

The poem "We are Seven" shows the impact of the humanism of Enlightenment. The poem, based on a real-life experience of Wordsworth's, explores the contrast between adult rationality and a child's logic. The narrator asks a little village girl about her siblings. The girl says that there are seven of them, including two who are dead. He tries to persuade her that her two deceased siblings cannot be counted among them because they are no longer alive. However, she insists that they can and must. For the narrator death is a fact that cannot be ignored, but the little girl will accept neither his mathematics nor his belief in the finality of death. He may ask rhetorically what an innocent child can know of death but the fact is that she does know what death is, for it has been close to her. This is not just a case of simplicity or innocence on the part of a child who wants to deny the fact of death, but the child's ability to go beyond the loss of death to an understanding of eternal life; for her the siblings are still alive through her love for them and in the plants that now spring forth from their graves (37). Her world is thus very different from that of the narrator. The poem's humanism lies in this rejection of the sterile, conventional scholastic-like logic, which cannot understand any other kind of reasoning and sees things only in terms of black and white; it is the child who seems more mature, rational and accepting of life's complexities, and their inability to understand each other's perceptions of the relationship between life and death shows how limiting individual perceptions can be.

In the poem "Anecdote for Fathers" there is a similar rejection of conventional rationality. The narrator asks his five-year-old son which place he likes better, Kilve on the sea, where they had spend a holiday last spring, or their present home, Liswyn Farm. The boy after thinking it over answers that he prefers Kilve. The narrator is surprised, and asks why. Little Edward finds it difficult to justify his choice, and in the end looks up and sees the weathercock on the house-top. There he finds his reason: because "there was no weather-cock" (55) at Kilve. The father has learnt an important lesson from the child:

> O dearest, dearest boy! my heart
>
> For better lore would seldom yearn,
>
> Could I but teach the hundredth part
>
> Of what from thee I learn. (57-60).

The child's truth is superior to adult reason because it is fresh and intuitive; there is no need, in fact, of any logical reason at all.

In "Lines composed upon the Thames near Richmond", written in 1789 and published in 1798, and titled later

"Remembrance of Collins", also shows the influence of philosophical humanism on Wordsworth. Looking at the river, the poet wishes that other poets, too, were able to share the vision of its beauty, quietness and depth:

O glide, fair stream! for ever so,

Thy quiet soul on all bestowing,

Till all our mind for ever flow

As thy deep waters now are flowing. (5-8)

Even if they cannot, the river should continue to flow in the same way, so that it might reflect "The image of a poet's heart" (11). Collins, who had written a poem on the death of Thomson, also blessed this scene, even though he was never able to over come his grief but only managed to turn it into pity. The poet now prays that no other poet should experience the same pain. This empathy for another's pain is a humanistic trait.

"Expostulation and Reply" and "Tables Turned" are sometimes taken in conjunction because of the similarity of their themes — the futility of bookish knowledge as compared to the lessons from Nature. Both these poems reveal a humanism of the philosophical kind. In the "Expostulation and Reply" the poet's friend, Matthew, spend more time reading and less time sitting outside and daydreaming, as if her were Mother Earth's "As if you were her first-born birth,/ And none had lived before you!" (11-12). Men who do not read are "forlorn and blind" (6). The poet's "reply" in stanzas five to seven expresses the belief of the Romantics that Nature and human intuition impart a knowledge and wisdom that cannot be found in books or in formal education: Nature nurtures the mind with a wisdom of its own. If Matthew's "expostulation" represents the neo-classical faith in enlightened reason, the poet's "reply' represents the Romantic preference for the powers of Nature. It is not through pursuing intellectual excellence but through submission to Nature that wisdom can be attained. Thus, though the poem is about the importance of Nature to human beings, its real subject is not Nature but humanity and how human beings learn, and thus belongs to the humanistic tradition. Thus the poem complements "The Tables Turned". The poet "turns the tables" on his friend, insisting that men should learn from nature instead of books. There is no doubt some irony in the fact that Wordsworth communicates this idea through the written medium himself.

The poem "Lines written at a small distance from my House, and sent by my little boy to the person to whom they are addressed" reveals a humanism of the philosophical kind. The poem is addressed to his sister Dorothy and has also been anthologized as "To my Sister". It repeats the Romantic belief in the importance of rejecting routine and reasoning for spontaneity and idleness:

> One moment now may give us more
>
> Than years of toiling reason;
>
> Our minds shall drink at every pore
>
> The spirit of the season.
>
> Some silent laws our hearts will make. (25-29)

The poet asks his sister to forsake her books and routine, because it is only then that beings can learn to love (35-36). This rejection of utilitarian logic for the world of feeling is again a humanistic trait.

"The Last of the Flock" evinces Wordsworth's humanitarianism in its portrayal of the plight of the peasant who once had fifty sheep in his flock, which he loved and cared for like his own children. But he had to sell them off one by one in order to feed his children. As he did so he found he was also gradually losing his humanity as well :

To wicked deeds I was inclined,

And wicked fancies crossed my mind;

And every man I chanced to see,

I thought he knew some ill of me;

No peace, no comfort could I find,

No ease, within doors or without. (71-76).

Now he has only one lamb left, "the last of the flock", which he has to sell, and he finds it difficult not to cry. The poem is thus about the loss of language that is associated with emotional loss, and is not simply a one-dimensional story about a shepherd going to sell his last lamb.

"Lines written in Early Spring" also reveals Wordsworth's humanism. As the poet sits, a bird is singing a song and a beautiful landscape all around him, be is "In that sweet mood when pleasant thoughts/Bring sad thought to the mind (3-4). He sees how humanity is linked to Nature and this makes him ponder over. "What man has made of man" (8). Everything that is natural is beautiful and pleasure-giving man cannot enjoy these heavenly blessings, but instead indulges in activities that are harmful to him. The poem concludes with a refrain in a form of a rhetorical question, "Have I not reason to lament/What man has made of man?" (23-24)

As Jacobus writes:

> 'The Lines written in early spring' admits the world may not be one of harmony and love after all. The poem centres on a clash between the optimism of Wordsworth's creed and his awareness that the One Life leaves the problems of ordinary life unsolved" (97).

The ballad "The Complaint of a Forsaken Indian Woman" is a humanitarian one. Written in the popular tradition of "Red Indian" (then the commonly used name for Nature Americans) ballads, which were used frequently to suggest universal human values by seeing them against exotic or alien contexts, the poem is based on the belief that there was a "Red Indian" custom of abandoning sick people who were unable to keep up with the tribe on their journey. (Jacobus 192) An ailing woman has been abandoned by her tribe because she is ill. She is full of despair:

> My fire is dead : it knew no pain;
>
> Yet is it dead, and I remain;
>
> All stiff with ice and ashes lie;
>
> And they are dead, and I will die,
>
> When I was well, I wished to live.
>
> (11-15)

Now, deserted, she does not fear death, but she wishes that she had not given up so soon and had continued to follow her tribe. This is especially because she has had to give up her child:

> My child! they gave thee to another,

A woman who was not thy mother,

When from my arms may Babe they took,

On me how strangely did he look!

Through his whole body something ran,

A most strange working did I see;

As if he strove to be a man.

(31-37)

Jacobus writes:

Returning again and again to the fixed point of her approaching death, the Indian woman voices the contradiction between her stoicism and her longing for child and friends, between fatalism and rebellion contradictions which must persist while she remains alive. (201)

Another poem about a women's desertion is "The Mad Mother", which Wordsworth renamed "Her Eyes Were Wild"in 1815. The poem about a mother who has been forsaken by her husband and is left alone with her son, is the only source of joy to her and her inspiration to continue to live. The poem is in the form of a soliloquy with occasional addresses to her infant in her arms, whom she reassures she will take care of:

I'll teach my boy the sweetest things;

I'll teach him how the owlet sings,

My little babe! thy lips are still,

And thou hast almost sucked thy fill,

Where are thou gone, my own dear child ?

(81-85)

The mother's isolation and her dependence on this one human relationship makes this a humanistic poem. The intensity of her grief makes her confuse her feeling with joy :

'Sweet babe! they say that I am mad,

But nay, my heart is far too glad;

And I am happy when I sing

Full many a sad and doleful thing. . .'

(11-14)

The son needs her care, so she will give him the male protection that has been denied her. This suggests the complexity of mutual need when the poet points out how the mother protects her child, the child in turn saves his mother :

'Suck, little babe, oh suck again!

It cools my blood; it cools my brain. . .' (31-32)

'Oh! love me, love me, little boy!

Thou art mother's only joy. . . (41-42)"

Havely has contrasted this poem with Goldsmith's "The deserted village" where Goldsmith feels great compassion for the wretched woman:

But from a distance. He doesn't get inside her suffering and by calling her the "historian" he is assigning her a role which she couldn't possibly understand. The same distancing is clear in his attitude to all the other former inhabitants : he makes no distinction in the amount of attention he gives to the watchdog and the village simpleton. It is significant that only the plain is given the quality of thought, not the people who live on it. Wordsworth on the other hand doesn't give the people he writes about the false dignity of calling them 'historians'. His respect is more real than assumed. He gets inside the people he writes about". (26)

"Simon Lee, Tale of an old Huntsman" is a poem about an old hunter whose poverty forces him to work hard even at the age of eighty, when he is already infirm. Once he was a youth now he depends on his wife Ruth. One day the poet was passing by his abode when he was trying to remove the root of a tree, seeing him unable to do it, the poet offers to help and receives much gratitude from Simon Lee. The poem focuses on the pathos of poverty and old age, and as Jacobus writes, extends "our sympathies – much as the literature of sensibility had done— by revealing that the humblest episodes of everyday life have a bearing on the human condition" (207). Jones and Tydeman also note:

> By embracing Simon in the universal bond of compassion, Wordsworth alters significantly the reader's point of view so that he is an object of human tragedy, not a subject of inhuman absurdity. It is not Simon but the reader who is changed, and the change is demonstrably attributable to the enlargement and refinement of our sensibilities. (20)

Thus it has been seen how in the poems of the LB of 1798 Wordsworth has used humanitarianism along with the philosophical humanism of the Renaissance and the Enlightenment. Out of nineteen poems written by Wordsworth in the first edition of the LB in 1978 only seventeen poems were analysed and two were left out because they were not included in the Complete Poetical Works of William Wordsworth edited by Thomas Hutchinson, namely "Female Wagrant" and "Old Traveller" which have been discussed in their longer versions, "Salisbury Plain" and "Cumberland Beggar" respectively.

Works Cited

Abrams, M.H. and Harold Bloom, Eds. "Preface." By W. Wordsworth. The Norton Anthology of Literature. New York: W.W. Norton & Company, 1976. 84-88.

Alisson, Alexander and Barrow, eds. The Norton Anthology of Poetry. New York: W.W. Norton Corp. Ltd., 1983.

Coleridge, S.T. Biographia Literaria. Ed. J. Shawcross. London: Oxford University Press, 1962.

Friedman, Michael H. William Wordsworth and the Idea of Community. New York: Columbia UP., 1979.

Haveley, Cecily. Wordsworth The Age of Revolutions Units 13-14 Arts: A Second Level Course. Milton Keynes: The Open University Press, 1976.

Hutchinson, Thomas, ed. Poetical Works of Wordsworth. London: Oxford University Press, 1953.

Jacobus, Mary. Tradition and Experiment in the Lyrical Ballads, *1798*. London: Clarendon Press, 1976.

James, Downey. A Humanist Meets his waterloo. <www. communications.uwaterloo.ca>

Jones and Tydeman, ed. Letter Wordsworth; Lyrical Ballads. William Wordsworth. London: Mac Millian Ltd., 1972, 212.

Jones, R. and Tydeman, Ed. Advertisement to the first edition of the LB. William Wordsworth; Lyrical Ballads. William Wordsworth. London: Mac Millian Ltd., 1972, 1-4.

Jones, R. and Tydeman, Eds. Idiot Boy and Simonlee William Wordsworth; Lyrical Ballads. John. F. Danby. London: Mac Millian Ltd., 1972, 205.

4

Humanism in the Lyrical Ballads : 1800

The poems analysed in this chapter are from the second edition of the LB in 1800.

The celebrated poem "Lucy Gray" is about a young girl Lucy who was lost in the snowy wilderness. The poet had heard her sad tale and the story that people sometimes hear her spirit singing a solitary song. This is again a poem of grief and loss and thus marks the poet's humanism.

"Lines written when sailing in a Boat at Evening" is a companion poem to "Lines written near Richmond, upon the Thames, at Evening" of 1798 edition. As the boat goes westward, the poet notices how the stream behind, which had seemed all lit up, by the sunset when he was nearing it, now seems dark. He relates this to the human condition:

Such views the youthful Bard allure;

But, heedless of the following gloom,

He deems their colours shall endure

Till peace go with him to the tomb. (9-12)

But it is better to live in hope in spite of the possibility of "grief and pain" (16) ahead. The relationship of the landscape to human destiny makes the humanism of this poem.

"The Pet-Lamb" is called a pastoral by Wordsworth. It describes the relationship between a mountain lamb and a little girl. Both the girl and the lamb are above, and the child is attempting to feed the lamb. Overbearing her talking to the lamb, the poet learns that the lamb was picked up by her father from the mountain and brought home, because its mother was dead. The lamb does not feed because it is missing its mother and tries to run away: "Why bleat so after me? Why pull so at thy chain?/Sleep—and at break of day I will come to thee again!" (59-60). The poet empathizes with both the lamb and the littlie girl.

The humanism behind the five "Lucy" poems, "She Dwelt among the untrodden ways", "Three years she grew", "Strange fits of passion I have known" and "A Slumber did my spirit seal" lies in the quality of love. Who the real Lucy is a matter of conjecture, but the poetic Lucy is the symbol of love and loss:

She lived unknown, and few could know

When Lucy ceased to be;

But she is in her grave, and, oh,

The difference to me !

("She Dwelt among the untrodden ways" 9-12)

These poems relate human life to natural processes :

No motion has she now, no force;
She neither hears nor sees;
Rolled round in earth's diurnal course,
With rocks, and stones and trees.

(A Slumber did my spirits seal, 5-8)

In "Three Years she Grew," the poet once again refers to Nature as the ideal teacher. But when Lucy achieves, perfection she dies, and becomes one with Nature. The poem is thus an example of Enlightenment humanism.

In the "Lucy" poem "Strange Fits of Passion" the lover suddenly and strangely imagines that his beloved, Lucy is going to die, a fear that is against logic and rationality. Havely's comment is relevant:

This poem is much more than a simple reaction against rationalism. It suggests the importance of acknowledging the mystery of the mind, not those of its aspects which are open to investigation. (30)

"The Two April Mornings" presents a conversation between a schoolmaster, Matthew, and the poet. It is a beautiful spring morning, spring being the season of the awakening of new life, but the schoolmaster cannot help sighing, because it was on a similar. April morning that he had buried his nine-year-old daughter Emma. Looking up after burying her he sees another young girl, happy and carefree, and is filled with pain, though he cannot wish that she were his daughter (55-6)

As Haveley remarks, in "Strange Fits of Passion" and "The Two April Mornings". "The explanation of Matthew's words was to be found in the way they related to an important factor in the poem which was not ostensibly its subject that is, the mood of joy". (Haveley 29)

In "The Fountain" there is a conversation between the poet and his schoolmaster friend Matthew, that is, between youth and old age (for Mathew is seventy-two). When the poet suggest that they talk about things and watch the beauty of their surroundings, the cheerful old man begins by comparing the flow of the stream from the spring near them to the progress of human life. Nothing can stop the "merry" (22) flow of the water, which will continue for a thousand years in the same way. He remembers the times when as a man in his prime he used lie down in the same way beside the spring and hear the same musical sound of the water. Now he is old and has lost so much through the years, and that he believes it is wiser to celebrate what he still has rather than to mourn what he has lost, just like the birds who do not try to fight against time and the laws of Nature. Human beings, however, are

And often, glad no more

We wear a face of joy, because

We have been glad of yore. (46-48)

He himself is close to death, and his happiness lies in remembering all his loved ones whom he has lost. The poet tries to assure Matthew that he will be a son to him, but knows someone else can never fill that gap. As they leave the fountain Mathew sings:

He sang those witty rhymes

About the crazy old church-clock,

And the bewildered chimes. (70-72)

The Lines which the poet had composed and referred to at the beginning of the poem.

"The Childless Father" is about Timothy, whose the last of children had died less than six months ago. His grief is contrasted with the gaiety of Nature around him and the festive mood of the village girls at the hunt. Timothy has to go out and join the hunt. He locks the door slowly, perhaps thinking as he does so that he has to do so because his daughter is not there to look after the house. But he says nothing to the poet, and simply goes to the chase "with a tear on his cheek" (20).

Wordsworth's editor classify "Hart-Leap Well" and such poems like "The Brothers and Michael" on the basis of the emotion they convey and it is their focus on the human values and common human feeling that makes these poems humanistic.

"Hart-Leap Well" composed in 1797 recounts the story of the hunt behind the name given to this spring. The Knight, Sir Walter, pursues the hunted deer so hard that all the hounds and the other hunters are exhausted cannot follow him. In the end he sees with joy that the hart is lying dead of exhaustion, with his nose touching the spring-waters as for sustenance and help, and he is amazed at the power of the deer that it was able to leap to this spot. He decides to build a pleasure-house thee and a small amour, and to commemorate the "gallant Stag" (65) decides to call the place 'Hart-Leap well' and to build a monument there.

The main thrust of the poem is contained in the second part of the poem. The poet in his travels comes across these monuments, and sees that it is all in a state of decay, from the building to the trees. A passing Shepherd tells him why it so and what has happened. No animal can drink from that spring in which the hart had breathed his last, from where "a dolorous groan" often comes out. Obviously a murder has been committed here- the murder of the hart which loved the place so much that he chose to die there. As a result the entire place has fallen into decay and despair. The poet agrees that its death "was mourned by sympathy divine" (164), and concludes:

> The being that is in the clouds and are,
>
> That is in the green leaves among the groves,
>
> Maintains a deep and reverential care
>
> For the unoffending creatures whom he loves. (165-8).

The lesson he has learnt is: "Never to blend our pleasure or our pride/With sorrow of the meanest thing that feels" (179-80).

"The Brothers" also evinces humanism by its focus on human values. The poem is about a sailor Leonard who migrates from his village in order to earn a livelihood for himself and his brother James. He comes back to the village to join his brother and to resume a country life. He meets the priest of the village in the churchyard, who does not recognize him.

The priest begins to tell him about the dead in the churchyard. When he comes to the grave of Leonard's grandfather Walter Ewebank, he tells him how he had taken care of his two grandchildren. But when the grandfather dies, all his property had to be sold off in order to pay his debts. Poor Leonard had to leave for the seas at the age of sixteen for the sake of his brother James, whom he leaves behind. The priest then tells him of the great bond between the two brothers; there was great love and affection between them and the elder one always did what he could for the younger one, even carrying him across the flooded river when necessary. The villagers are sure that Leonard is now a slave of the Moors, and will never return.

When Leonard asks the priest about James, he is informed that, James had become very lonely and villagers took good care of him. His health deteriorated and he developed somnambulism. One day he disappeared and could not be found. In the end his body was discovered under the 'pillar', a high rock formation. Overcome by grief and loss, Leonard now leaves the village and his dreams forever.

"Michael" is humanistic in a similar way. Wordsworth in his childhood had heard the tale of Michael from an eighty-years-old shepherd, who remained strong and sturdy, he had a sixty-year-old wife, Isabella, and an eighteen-year-old only son, Luke. Michael adored his little son and looked after him like a mother, and in his old age the boy was "his comfort and his daily hope" (206)

One day they were shocked to receive summons to discharge the forfeiture of their property, which he had offered as surety for his nephew. Now Michael had to sell a part of his property, and Luke was sent to another thriving kinsman to earn some money. The day before he goes to the city, Michael takes him to the sheep fold that they had planned, and asks Luke to lay the foundation stone.

Once in the city, however, Luke balls into evil ways and finally has to escape overseas Michael is completely shattered and soon after he dies. Isabel too dies shortly afterwards, and their property is sold. All that remains is the unfinished sheep-fold. Again it is the human feeling behind this common tale of the lives of ordinary people that makes the poem humanistic.

"To a Sexton" addresses the village sexton tilling the graves and gathering the bones. The gloomy work of the sexton is in fact like a gardener's. The gardener glories in his beautiful flowers, while the sexton tends the dead, but his garden is far superior, because he deals with human hearts and feeling. Human being are thus more valuable than Nature's gifts.

"The Reverie of Poor Susan" too is humanist in the same way. Whenever the poor Susan passes by, a caged thrush in a city street whom she hears sings, she remembers the happiness of her past in the countryside: "And a river flows on through the vale of Cheapside" (8). But she soon awakens to reality and the loss of her past.

"A Whirl-Blast from Behind the Hill", composed in 1798 and published in 1800, reveals a humanism more characteristic of the Renaissance. The poem describes the aftermath of a storm, when the hail falls leaves which jump about in the wind. They seem to the poet to be dancing merrily to the tune of a medieval folk song. Thus a poem about destruction and decay becomes one of happiness, and optimism which were some of the characteristic features of the Renaissance humanism.

"Rural Architecture" reveals a philosophical humanism. Three village schoolboys build a man of stone on the peak of a crag and call him "Ralph Jones" (11) who was known in the Legberthwaite valley for his strength of bones as the

"Magog" (12). A week later, a strong winds "blew the giant away" (16). Undeterred the boys built another one. The poet is impressed by their indomitable spirit, and sees in their endeavour an inspiration.

Wordsworth's attack on the Catholics is reminiscent of the humanism of the Renaissance :

> Some little I've seen of blind boisterous works
>
> By Christian disturbers more savage than Turks,
>
> Spirits busy to do and undo;
>
> At remembrance whereof my blood sometimes will flag.
>
> (19-22)

The Wandering few is an archetypal symbol of quest, and "The Song of the Wandering Jew" contains the humanism of the Renaissance in its search for the answers regarding things around us. Similarly, "The Oak and the Broom" reveals Renaissance humanism. The Andrew, the shepherd has learnt from Nature a truth that he shares with his family. A tall and sturdy oak tree—a traditional symbol of strength and permanence—warns the little broom plant at its feet to move, because it is sure that the frost that had rent so many of the neighbouring rocks would destroy it. But the broom refuses to heed the warning for thus place is where he belongs: "And he is oft the wisest man,/Who is not wise at all. (63-4). In the end it is the mighty oak that is fallen by the storm, Oak, warns the little when a piece of rock was about to fell on the broom by catching it.

"A Poet's Epitaph" reveals Wordsworth's philosophical humanism. The poet's soul admonishes the visitors at his grave—the politician, the lawyer, the doctor, the soldier the moralist, the intellectual—not to waste their time at his burial place; only the man who loves Nature is contented with little, and has "The harvest of a quiet eye/That broods and sleeps of his own heart" (51-2) should go to him, because:

> Impulses of deeper birth
>
> Have come to him in solitude. (47-48)

The sentiment is clearly humanist one.

"The Old Cumberland Beggar" is an extension of "The Old Man Travelling". Wordsworth was inspired to write about this beggar from one whom he used to see since his childhood. The poem is about an old beggar who sits at the foot of a hill and depends on the alms offered by the villagers and the passers by to keep his body and soul together.

Godwin had said that a beggar was a useless product of corrupt society; in a better society all such would be fed and sheltered and required to work. He also included beggars in his list of the socially useless who should be removed out of way of society's progress. But Wordsworth's beggar is useful to society:

> Tis Nature's law
>
> That none, the meanest of created things,
>
> Of forms created the most of vile and brute.
>
> The dullest or most noxious, should exist
>
> Divorced from good—a spirit and pulse of good,
>
> A live and soul, to every mode of being

Inseparably linked... (73-9)

Harold Bloom writes :

The Old Man performs many functions. The most important is that of a binding agent for the memories of good impulses in all around him. Wherever he goes.

(55)

The Beggar gives a chance to the poor and the destitute to help others:

The mild necessity of use compels

To acts of love ....

To virtue and true goodness.

(98-101)

Wordsworth thus goes against the rational alternative of the beggars being put into the workhouse. He wants them to enjoy freedom and Nature:

May never House, misnamed of Industry,

Make him a captive! for that pent-up din,

Those life-consuming sounds that clog the air,

Be his the natural silence of old age!

Let him be free of mountains solitudes;

And have around him, whether heard or not,

The pleasant melody of woodland birds.

(179-184)

Bloom has compared the description of the Cumberland Beggar with that of Tolstoy's beggar and says that "the Tolstoy's beggar is a sufferer; in Wordsworth he bears the mark of 'animal tranquillity and decay', the title given by Wordsworth to a fragment closely connected to the longer poem. In the fragment the Old Man travels on and moves not with pain, but with thought" (57).

"The Idle Shepherd Boys or, Dungeon-Ghyll Force" is about two shepherd boys Walter and James, sitting idly in the sun, who decide to run a race. Walter challenges James to cross the chasm of Dungeon-Ghyll with him. As they attempt to do so they hear the plaintive cry of a lamb which had slipped and fallen into the stream, while the ewe above stood crying.

The boys are aghast at the sight and are wondering how to rescue the lamb. Just then, they see a man who is a poet, picking up it from the stream. He returns it to them and they put him besides his mother. The poet chides the boys to "mind their trade". (99)

Once again it is in the portrayal of childhood and of human emotions that the poet's humanism lies.

"In the Waterfall and the Eglantine" is a dialogue between a waterfall and a plant through which Wordsworth expresses his views against oppression and injustice. The fall threatens the plant to move out of its way:

'Dost thou presume my course to block?

Off, off! or, puny Thing!

I'll hurl thee headlong with the rock

To which thy fibres cling.' (11-14)

Waterfall was a small cascade. The plant tries to reason with it, reminding it of their old relationship before it was so "Swollen with shows"(5), and promising to decorate it till the last. But the waterfall does not listen, and thunders down and drowns the plant.

Wordsworth's humanism is reflected in the rose's appeal for "peaceful co-existence and not to fight anymore.

The subject of "Andrew Jones" is an Unpleasant person who not only swears and drinks, but even worse than this who robs the poor crippled beggar of his money. The poet is sure Andrew's sons will be like him, and he wishes person who does not shy from stealing and his sons also follow his foot steps therefore Wordsworth would not mind if Andrew is banished from the village.

Wordsworth's humanitarianism in the poem "Ruth" reveals the poets philosophical humanism too. The young Ruth, neglected after her father remarries, finds happiness in wild Nature. When she grows up she meets a young soldier from America who represents for her the unknown world of freedom. They marry and are happy at first in domesticity. But the soldier wishes to return to his earlier life, and deserts Ruth, who goes mad with grief. It is her memories of Nature that help her, and finally she finds refuge in the wilderness "Under the greenwood tree" (215) – the echo from Shakespeare's As you Like It of the idyllic life in Arden suggesting how happy she is now, in spite of poverty, loneliness and age.

The importance of Nature is reinforced in the poem, as is the poet's humanitarianism. The last line, "A Christian psalm for thee" (258) is of particular interest because all through her life religion has meant nothing for her or did anything.

"The Two Thieves" also make use of Christian symbol in its title. The two thieves are three-year-old boy and his ninety-years-old grandfather, who always enjoyed stealing whenever they could. The poet realizes that he should not pity the old man, but love him. He says that there is so much to learn from him about human nature: "Long yet may'st thou live! for a teacher we see/That lifts up the veil of our nature in thee (47-48). The delight in their petty thievery, the absence of sense of blame attached to them, is foreshadow in the beginning of the poem, where books—representing conventional rationality—are rejected. This again, is a characteristic the Enlightenment of humanism.

In these forty-two poems of the LB of both 1798 and 1800 editions, it may be observed how felicitously Wordsworth has used tradition and experiment in expressing his humanism and which lies not only in his sympathetic treatment of the underprivileged but also in his rejection of Godwian rationalism and logic.

Jones and Tydeman write :

Wordsworth's later poetry indeed even the 1800 Lyrical Ballads, is more complex, more accomplished in is effects. Yet perhaps this voyage outwards to explore the world of elemental forces was a necessary preliminary to the long voyage within that is begun by 'Tintern Abbey' and continued in *The Prelude*. ...The 'experiment' to which he refers in the Advertisement of 1798 had been completed and was never repeated. (24)

Bloom writes on the subjects of the LB :

What led Wordsworth to the subject of human decay, to depictions of idiocy, desertion, beggars, homeless wanderers. He sought images of alienated life, as we might judge them, which he could see and present as images of natural communion. The natural man, free of consciousness in any of our senses, yet demonstrates a mode of consciousness, which both intends nature for its object and at length blends into that object.

(qtd. in Cowell 57)

Works Cited

Cowell, Raymond, Ed. "The Old Cumberland Beggar". By Harold Bloom. Critics on Wordsworth. New Delhi: Universal Book Stall, 1990. 55, 57.

Haveley, Cecily. Wordsworth The Age of Revolutions Units 13-14 Arts: A Second Level Course. Milton Keynes: The Open University Press, 1976.

Hutchinson, Thomas, ed. Poetical Works of Wordsworth. London: Oxford University Press, 1953.

Jacobus, Mary. Tradition and Experiment in the Lyrical Ballads, *1798.* London: Clarendon Press, 1976.

Jones and Tydeman, Eds. Of Trees and Men: The Unity Of Wordsworth's The Thorn. Wordsworth; Lyrical Ballads. by Albert S. Gerard. London: The Macmillan Press Ltd., 1972. 220.

5

Humanism in the Shorter Poems of Wordsworth

This chapter studies the humanism in Wordsworth's shorter poems, including his odes and sonnets. The poems would be discussed in the order of their composition, and exclude those referred to in the previous chapters.

As has been suggested earlier, a reading of the poems in the LB shows how Wordsworth in the LB uses the stories of grief and destitution, with their landscape of distress, ruins, inclement weather, and so on, for the purposes of humanitarian protest. His poetry, then, reveals what Jacobus calls his "commitment to the realities of human suffering" (134). Out of such writing comes his first major narrative poem, "Salisbury Plain", originally based on the story of "The Female Vagrant", a poem in the first edition of the L.B. in 1798. It was expanded into a new poem called "Guilt and Sorrow" and was published in the Poems, Chiefly of Early and Late Years in 1842.

"Salisbury Plain" is the most impressive protest poem of its time. Wordsworth wrote it in 1793, and later expanded and altered it to “Adventures on “Salisbury Plain” (1794) and finally to “Guilt and Sorrow; or, Incidents upon Salisbury Plain” Wordsworth noted in a letter that the purpose of the poem was to “expose the vices of penal law and the calamities of war as they affect individuals” (qtd. in Vincent). In “Salisbury Plain” the Female Vagrant’s story of the LB is subordinated to a more complex narrative that centres on a good man driven by injustice to murder. The Female Vagrant has now become the Soldier’s Widow, and the narrator’s encounter with her is one of the strongest indictments of the British Government’s policies against the poor and the homeless. The Soldier’s Widow and the Sailor are equally victims, even though the Sailor becomes a murderer. He does, however, meet his wife in the end, only to have her die in front of him, and he is finally caught and hanged, just as he himself has seen a hanged man upon the deserted and brooding Salisbury Plain. This legendary site of the ancient Druids, with its stark landscape and its brooding altars in Stonehenge, becomes a metaphor for the inability of religion and conventional society to take care of the marginalized and the subaltern. Thus the poem is both a humanitarian one and an example of philosophical humanism.

Jacobus writes about the tragic overtones of the poem:

Dispossession first, then the ravages of war, precipitate her into dependence on a precarious family happiness, and finally into the unrelieved despair with which the second part of the poem is largely concerned. With this second part, ‘A Night on Salisbury Plain’ emerges as a forerunner-however crude— of Wordsworth’s mature studies of suffering. The narrative sweeps relentlessly towards, not disaster, but its aftermath, alienation. (148-149)

"Peter Bell" was started in the summer of 1798 and was published in 1819. The poem has been described as "emphatically humane" (Jacobus 265). Peter Bell is a potter by profession. He is a wicked character, who has led a "lawless life" (276) to begin with, but his character is transformed at the end of the poem. One day he goes on a trip on the back of his horse, during which he experiences certain supernatural events, and he repents. His redemption starts when he remembers his sixth wife and cries for her. He feels for mankind as he never felt before. His redemption is completed when he shares the agony of a widow and her child:

> And Peter Bell the ruffian wild
>
> Sobs loud, he sobs just like a child,
>
> 'Oh! God, I can endure no more!' (1118-20)

Parallels can be drawn between Coleridge's "ancient mariner" and "Peter Bell". Both the poems have the same moral; for the mariner it is in the form of a prayer, but for Peter Bell, as Jacobus suggests, it is the "capacity for tears that matters, not prayer. Weeping in Peter Bell serves as an index of humanity" (265).

"Alice Fell, or Poverty" was composed on March 12, 13, 1802 and published in 1807. The narrator is travelling in a post-chaise on a windy night when he suddenly hears a pitiful moan. He searches for the source of the sound and finally discovers a little girl sitting all alone in the cart and crying bitterly, who can only utter "My cloak!" (21). He finds that her cloak is entangled in the wheel of the cart:

A Weather-beaten rag as e'er

From any garden scare-crow dangled.

There, twisted between nave and spoke,

It hung, nor could at once be freed,

But our joint pains unloosed the cloak,

A miserable rag indeed!

(27- 32)

When he asks her where she is going all alone on these lonely ways, and what brings her into the chaise with him, she tells him her story: that her name is Alice Fell, that she is an orphan and belongs to Durham. But she is weeping not because she is an orphan but because her cloak is ruined, and "She wept, nor would be pacified" (52). The narrator reaches the girl at the tavern and asks the innkeeper to buy her a new cloak with the money he gives him. The new cloak gave the little girl a new sense of pride and self-esteem.

"I travelled among unknown men" is one of the Lucy poems and was composed in 1801 and published in 1807. As the poet travels abroad "among unknown men" (1) his distance from Lucy brings home to him his love not only for Lucy but also for his country.

Among thy mountains did I feel

The joy of my desire;

And she I cherished turned her wheel

Beside an English fire.

Thy mornings showed, thy nights concealed,

The bowers where Lucy played;

And thine too is the last green field

That Lucy's eyes surveyed.

(9-16)

Lucy's death charges his memories of the landscape of his home with emotion. The humanitarianism of the poem lies in the poet's merging of the natural landscape with humanity and with human emotion. The philosophical humanism of the renaissance lies in the patriotism of the poet:

"Resolution and Independence or The Leech-Gatherer" (1807) reveals both humanitarianism as well as philosophical humanism. The poem begins with the narrator brooding over the inevitability of death and the "vain and melancholy" ways of men (21):

To me that morning did it happen so;

And fears and fancies thick upon me came;

Dim sadness-and blind thoughts, I knew not, nor could name. (26-28)

This is in stark contrast with the happiness that Nature exudes:

All things that love the sun are out of doors;

The sky rejoices in the morning's birth;

The grass is bright with rain—drops;-on the moors

The hare is running races in her mirth;

And with her feet she from the plashy earth

Raises a mist; that, glittering in the sun,

Runs with her all the way, wherever she doth run. (8-14)

He thinks of his own fate and compares himself with Chatterton and Burns:

We Poets in our youth begin in gladness;

But thereof come in the end despondency and madness. (48-49)

It is at this time that he sees an old man who is so intent on his leech-gathering that he seems to be a part of Nature itself:

As a huge stone is sometimes seen to lie

Couched on the bald to of an eminence. (58-59)

He is so old and so bent with suffering that the poet cannot help talking to him. When the old man answers that he is transformed by the strength of human dignity, and his words sound like:

Choice word and measured phrase, above the reach

Of ordinary men; a stately speech;

Such as grave Livers do in Scotland use,

Religious men, who give to God and man their dues. (95-98)

He becomes for the poet a symbol of the power of human endeavour, independence, and survival which are characteristics of the Renaissance Humanism:

'God', said I, 'be my help and stay secure;

I'll think of the Leech-gatherer on the lonely moor!" (139-140)

Thus the old man gives courage and strength to live on.

"My Heart Leaps Up" was composed in March 1802 and published in 1807. When the poet sees a rainbow his "heart leaps up" with joy, for the rainbow is a traditional symbol of hope and survival, characteristics of the Renaissance Humanism his own joyous response to the rainbow has continued since his childhood and he knows that in spite of maturity and the nearness of death it will continue to inspire him. In fact, the day he does not react to the rainbow in the same way it will be as good as death for him. The poem concludes with the philosophical lines:

The Child is father of the Man;

And I could wish my days to be

Bound each to each by natural piety. (7-9)

A similar belief faith is expressed also in his famous "Immortality Ode" with its echo of the Platonic belief in pre-existence. The humanism of the poem becomes evident in the last two lines in particular, with the mention of "natural piety".

The above lines are repeated as an epigraph to "The Ode on Intimations of Immortality From Recollections of

Early Childhood" (popularly known as the "Immortality Ode" 1807). This poem, with its Platonic and neo-Platonic overtones, may be read as an example of the impact of Renaissance humanism upon the poet. The account of the period of childhood as one of unalloyed bliss, which gradually disappears as he grows older, may be found in other Romantic poets too, such as Coleridge's ("Frost at Midnight" and "Dejection").

> And not in utter nakedness,
>
> But trailing clouds of glory do we come
>
> From God, who is our home. (64-66)

In neo-Platonic fashion, the poet believes that just as Nature compensates for the child's banishment from "the glory do we come"(64):

> Earth fills her lap with pleasures of her own;
>
> Yearnings she hath in her own natural kind,
>
> And, even with something of a Mother's mind,
>
> And no unworthy aim,
>
> The homely Nurse doth all she can
>
> To make her foster child, her Inmate Man,
>
> Forget the glories he hath known,
>
> And that imperial place whence he came. (77-84)

His distance from his childhood has brought about a gradual decay of belief in immortality, for earthly existence is weighed down with the weight of "custom": "Heavy as frost, and deep almost as life!" (129-30) .

Nevertheless, he knows that he is not entirely bereft, for:

O joy! that in our embers

Is something that doth live,

That nature yet remembers

What was so fugitive. (131-34)

This is evident in

Those obstinate questionings

Of sense and outward things

Falling from us, vanishings

Blank misgivings of a Creature

Moving about in world not realized,

High instincts before which our mortal nature

Did tremble like a guilty Thing surprised. (143-49)

Most important is the fact that the memories of the past are:

yet the fountain light of all our day,

Are yet a master light of all our seeing. (154-55).

Besides, even though the adult has lost much of his early vision he can find:

Strength in what remains behind;
In the primal sympathy
Which having been must ever be;
In the soothing thoughts that spring
Out of human suffering;
In the faith that looks through death,
In years that bring the philosophic mind. (182-88)

The poem shows both Renaissance humanism and the influence of the Enlightenment in the faith in the child's ability to grow and transform himself, as well as in its search for knowledge.

"Those words were uttered as in pensive mood", published in 1807, reveals a humanism characteristic of much of the eighteenth century. In the Epigraph to the poem, Wordsworth seems to have the 'Immortality Ode' in mind, because he alludes to the "heavenly utterances" that seem to fade away with the passage of time. The sonnet once again points to the poet's growth from the sensuous but transitory delights of Nature to an intellectual joy in the permanence of the objects of the human mind. No matter how beautiful Nature is, he cannot "disparage Man's gifts" (8), and realizes that:

These cleave to it; from these it cannot roam,
Nor they from it: their fellowship is secure. (13-14)

It is here that the poem's humanism lies.

The sonnet invocation to Milton in "London, 1802" is evidence of the influence of the humanism of the Renaissance. Milton was a republican and a humanist:

So didst thou travel on life's common way,

In cheerful godliness; and yet thy heart

The lowliest duties on herself did lay. (12-14)

Moreover, what Wordsworth, and Milton before him, desired for the English people were the humane and humanist qualities of "manners, virtue, freedom, power" (8) which were the characteristics of the Renaissance Humanism.

"Composed upon Westminister Bridge, September 3, 1802" (1807) a sonnet, which is also an example of the influence of the humanism of the Renaissance. Looking out at the city of London from this famous, Bridge, the poet is moved not by the glory of the wild countryside, as in several of his other poems, but of the city:

This City now doth, like a garment, wear

The beauty of the morning; silent, bare,

Ships, towers, domes, theatres, and temples lie

Open unto the fields, and to the sky. (4-7)

Indeed, from the distance the city, with all its signs of human use and habitation— "Ships, towers, domes, theatres, and temples lie"(6)— seems even more beautiful and calm than a natural scene untouched by humanity:

Never did sun more beautifully steep

In this first splendour, valley, rock, or hill;

Ne'er saw I, never felt, a calm so deep! (9-11).

That serenity can lie even within the heart of a bustling centre of human activity is a mark of the poet's belief in humanity and of his humanism.

The same serenity may be found in "It is a beauteous evening", composed in August 1802 and published, like many of his other sonnets, in the 1807 volume. The evening to him is a "holy time" that:

The holy time is quiet as a Nun

Breathless with adoration" (2-3).

The comparison of the time to humanity is ofcourse humanistic. The sun may set, but:

Listen! the mighty Being is awake,

And doth with his eternal motion make

A sound like thunder— everlastingly. (6-8)

But the meaning of this holy quiet and calm atmosphere becomes evident not in the natural surroundings which make it obvious but in the human presence there. Addressing the "Dear Child! dear Girl!" (9), who is there with him, the poet remarks that even if the child seems "untouched by solemn thought,/Thy nature is not therefore less divine" (10-11), because true holiness lies in the human spirit and not in any external worship:

Thou liest in Abraham's bosom all the year

And worshipp'st at the Temple's inner shrine,

God being with thee when we know it not. (12-14).

In this connection Dowden's comments from the Aldine Edition of Wordsworth's poems of 1892, quoted by Hutchinson in his Notes, are relevant: "But there are glad childlike hearts untouched by great solemnities, yet pure and sacred: mystery of the sea" (qtd. in Hutchinson 704). It is this belief that makes this poem a humanistic one.

"The World Is Too Much with Us" (1807) highlights the importance of Nature in moulding a person's character. The poet says that people become indifferent to the beauties of Nature, which have many things to convey, but under the weight of the world people do not pay heed to Nature. As has been seen earlier, Nature was an important part of Enlightenment humanism. Wordsworth's longing for the pagan sense of wonder is a mark of humanism.

"The Solitary Reaper" contains humanism of the humanitarian kind. It was composed in November 1805 and published in 1807 and is a poem about a young Highland lass whose song was heard by Wordsworth in the mountains of Scotland while he was on the tour of the country.

The girl is singing a sad song and Wordsworth imagines what could be the reasons for the girl's rendering of such a doleful song; he imagines was it a war in which she lost her dear ones that made her sing such a sad tune while she was cutting the corps with a sickle, or is the song about old things or is it about "some familiar matter of today"? (22)

or it is some more humble lay, ...

Some natural sorrow, loss, or pain,

That has been, and may be again ? (21-24)

"The Affliction of Margaret" composed in 1804 and published in 1807 contains humanitarianism as well as humanism of Enlightenment. The poem is the dramatic monologue of a mother whose only son has been missing for seven years. She yearns for him to come back to her, no matter what he has done or wherever he is, because she loves him in spite of every thing.

The son cannot guess what is it like to a mother to lose her child:

He knows it not, he cannot guess:

Years to a mother bring distress;

But do not make her love the less. (26-28)

She pleads with him:

Then come to me, my Son, or send

Some tidings that my woes may end;

I have no other earthly friend!

(26-28)

The sonnet "On The Extinction Of The Venetian Republic", composed in August 1802 and published in 1807 depicts humanism of the Renaissance. The poem once again evinces Wordsworth's faith in liberty. It expresses his Sorrow at the fate of the republic of Venice, taken over by Napolean Bonaparte in 1797, and thus losing its pre-eminent position as:

> the eldest Child of Liberty,/
>
> ... a maiden City, bright and free;
>
> (4-5).

Even though cities, like human beings, must decay, it is but natural that they should be lamented over: "Men that which once was great is passed away." (13-14)

"Stepping West ward" composed in June 1805 and published in 1807 evinces the humanism of the Renaissance. The poem is a conversation between Wordsworth, his travelling companion and the two women during a tour near Loch Ketterine. The soft questioning by one of the women makes him thing:

> The echo of the voice inwrought
>
> A human sweetness with the thought
>
> Of travelling through the world that lay
>
> Before me in my endless way.
>
> (23-26)

The religious sonnet "From The Same. To The Supreme Being" composed in 1805 and published in 1807, also shows Renaissance humanism. In the sonnet the poet says that without the aid of God his heart is like "Barren Clay" (3) He prays to God, the father, to lead and show him how to "unbind" "the fetters of [his] tongue (12):

That I may have the power to sing of Thee,

And sound thy praises everlastingly.

(13-14)

Therefore, Wordsworth solicits the God whom he calls the 'Supreme Being' to endow him with the virtues which he can lead his life on the footsteps of the Supreme Being.

The sonnet "Where lies the Land to which yon Ship must go?" (1807) and evinces the humanism of the Enlightenment. The ship becomes a metaphor for human life. It does not care where it goes, but crosses the sea regardless. The poet watches the ship's leaving, and concludes:

...some thing dark,

Of the old Sea some reverential fear,

Is with me at thy farewell, joyous Bark!

(12-14)

Incidentally, it may be seen how the poem rejects the rational idea that everything and every person must have a definite goal.

"Methought I saw the footsteps of a throne" (1807) displays Renaissance humanism. The sonnet is addressed to Death, who is like a king, because it rules over all of human life. As the poet climbs the footsteps of the throne of Death; he sees among the dead a beautiful young girl. This brings to him home, the truth of the brevity of youth and beauty.

"Surprised by joy" was composed in June 1812 and published in 1815 and contains humanism of the Renaissance. The sonnet describes the poet's feelings for his second daughter Catherine who died at the age of three.

The poet wants to share his every joy with his late daughter by sitting at her grave. Nothing was more important and precious in the world to Wordsworth than his daughter. No happenings of fate can change the spot of her grave nor the poet's love for his daughter - it was the worst hour in his life when he got separated forever from his daughter.

> Was the worst pang that sorrow ever bore,
>
> Save one, one only, when I stood forlorn,
>
> Knowing my heart's best treasure was no more;
>
> That neither present time, nor years unborn.
>
> (10-13)

"The Shepherd, looking eastward, softly said" was composed (?) and published in 1815 and also evinces humanism of the Renaissance. In the sonnet the poet describes a Shepherd's thoughts regarding moon when the former beholds it.

The Shepherd marvels at the radiant moon but then it gets covered with a cloud leaving darkness around the moon, but celestial body that once was proud of its beauty is contented with the "triumph of modest pride" (14).

In the poem Wordsworth highlights the virtue of modesty - the moon which once was proud if its beauty realises how a cloud can obscure its beauty and is satisfied that the cloud cannot completely hide him.

"From the dark chambers of dejection" was composed in 1814 and published in 1815 and evinces Renaissance humanism. In the sonnet Wordsworth writes that from the dark chambers of dejection, care becomes free. In the poem the poet suggests that the poetry celebrates a cheerful life with the human spirit soaring in delight. The poem punctuates the quality of joy and optimism which were the qualities of the Renaissance humanism.

A cheerful life is what the Muses love,

A soaring spirit is their prime delight.

(13-14)

"Grief, thou hast lost an ever-ready friend" was composed in (?) and published in 1819 shows yet again humanism of Renaissance. In the sonnet Wordsworth tells that grief or sorrow could be alleviated by care, love and joy. Love influences more in soothing a grief stricken heart than the music of flute. Even joy has the power to assuage the nerves of a sorrowful heart. It exerts a spiritual influence to bless a grievous soul:

Assiduously to soothe her aching breast;

And, to a point of just relief, abate

The mantling triumphs of a day too blest.

(12-14)

Love and Joy form the important attributes of the Renaissance humanism.

"Composed in one of the valleys of Westmoreland, on Easter Sunday" was composed (?) and published in 1819 also evinces humanism of humanitarianism as well as humanism of Renaissance. In the sonnet the poet describes the simple and humble rural life. The poem opens with the description of a rustic girl wearing home spun woollen cloth. It seems to the poet as if the wool while it was being sheared it paid homage to the "Prince of Peace" (7) that is, Christ. He says that when there were no artistic inventions that made life comfortable, people took benefits from nature's gifts and the "Benefits were weighed in Reason's scales !" (14)

The above mentioned line of the sonnet suggest a tilt in favour of reason which was a characteristic of the Enlightenment humanism. The poem also speaks of many humane attributes such as simple rural life and peace, suggestive of humanitarianism.

"I watch, and long have watched, with calm regret" was composed in (?) and published in 1819 and also shows humanism of the Renaissance. In the sonnet the poet contrasts the brightness of the Sun with the deteriorating life of humans. Wordsworth says that the Sun is the most shining star of the firmament or quire and over shines its compeers or God or angels, while after setting down the Sun rises once again to its glory but man once fallen finds it very difficult to rise up from his decline and it seems to Wordsworth that no beams can restore man's fate.

"I heard alas! twas only in a dream" was composed in (?) and published in 1819 also contains humanism of Renaissance. The sonnet is inspired from 'Phedo' of Plato. In the poem Wordsworth imagines to here verses from antiquity which seems to him carried from a wind from the lake or stream. The harmony of the verses is match by the billows created by the swan who is the "votary of the Apollo" (I heard alas! twas only in a dream, 9) and whose song inspires in contrast to a man's verse which is hardly inspiring. The humanism of the poem lies in the quality of the inspiration, which was the one of the features of the Renaissance humanism.

"Why Minstrel, these untuneful murmurings" composed in (?) and published in 1827 evinces humanism of the humanitarian kind, in which the poet highlights the function of poetry in service of mankind. The sonnet is addressed to a minstrel who is singing a jarred note. Wordsworth tells her that the poetry springs forth from the :

..... fountain of the heart,

The Poetry of Life and all that Art

Divine of words quickening insensate things.

(6-8)

Wordsworth pays a tribute to the innocent poets who have lost their lives for the just cause for whom:

Sun, moon and stars, all struggle in the toils

Of mortal sympathy;

(11-12)

Wordsworth writes that by rendering an unharmonious tune perhaps the minstrel also pays her homage to the poets who became martyrs.

"There is a pleasure in poetic pains" composed (?) and published in 1827 shows humanism of Renaissance. In the sonnet Wordsworth says that a poet undergoes lot of pains in composing a poem but his reward is the pleasure that he derives from it. Wordsworth writes that a poet is very happy to cleave to his ideals and principles despite all the obstacles and the hindrances.

Humanism in the poem lies in stating the true character of a poet who writes for the sake of humanity.

"To a snowdrop" composed (?) and published in 1819 also evinces Wordsworth's humanism of Renaissance. The sonnet is about reflections of Wordsworth when he sees a snowdrop which is on a flower that is as white as the snow. It gives him impression that it is fearful as to offend an uninvited guest when it bends itself. It seems to Wordsworth that the winds coming from the top of the mountains and the rising sun welcome the snowdrop as a friend whose spirit and enthusiasm seems to overrun May. Wordsworth finds the quality of grace in the snowdrop whom he considers as the "harbinger of spring" (To a snowdrop, 13).

Philosophical humanism of the poem lies in the qualities the poet gives to snowdrop such as that of courtesy, zeal and grace, which were the qualities of the Renaissance humanism.

"Fair prime of life" composed (?) and published in 1827 also shows humanism of Renaissance. In the sonnet Wordsworth suggests that a person should adjust with the adverse circumstances if he encounters them in the prime of his life. The adversities are symbolized by the gathering of clouds and mixing of weeds with the poppy flower.

Prime of life can be raised by its agents but :

Unpitied by the wise, all censure stilled,

Ah! show that worthier honours are thy due.

(7-8)

According to Wordsworth crime of life arouses deeper feelings in the heart. It inspires a man to think of sublime and loftier ideals and if any joy is ungrateful to the memory then that joy must be removed.

"To The Cuckoo" composed in (?) and published in 1827 evinces Wordsworth's humanism of Renaissance. In the sonnet Wordsworth shows the anodyne powers of the cuckoo which by its gladful song soothes the spirits of the captivc in the bounds of the four walls who counts his days to be still spent in the confinement; the song of the bird gives solace to a sick person.

Wordsworth pays high tribute to the bird when he says that there may a time come when an eagle will stop searching for its prey and there may not be the roar of a lion in the jungle but the wind will always carry the shrill of cuckoo when the spring arrives.

"Humanity" composed in 1829 and published in 1835 evinces Wordsworth's Enlightenment humanism and can be called summum bonum of Wordsworth's humanistic creed. The poem starts with the stones that were of religious and legal importance in the old days in Britain and Ireland. Once again one come across the importance of the function of poetry :

Enraptured Art draws from those sacred springs

Streams that reflect the poetry of things

Where Christian Martyrs stand in hues portrayed.

(18-21)

The poem evinces Wordsworth's views against tyranny, imperialism and in favour of equality of all the creatures. Wordsworth says that a person should exercise self restraint or forbearance and genius should not take pride :

> What a fair world were ours for verse to pains,
>
> If power could live at ease with self restraint!
>
> Opinion bow before the naked sense.
>
> (41-43)

The last line reveals Wordsworth's rejection of rationalism in favour of Lockian philosophy of senses. Wordsworth's rejection of rationalism is also seen earlier in the poem when he seems to believe in the power of stones to deliver justice and in the sayings of birds and winds :

> Yet, for the initiate, rocks and whispering trees
>
> Do still perform mysterious offices!
>
> And functions dweel in beast and bird that sway
>
> The reasoning mind, or with the fancy play.
>
> (9-12)

Wordsworth's views that British have different laws for themselves and different for those living overseas, smacks of colonization.

> Our varying moods, on human kind or brute,
>
> Twere well in little, as in great, to pause,

Lest Fancy trifle with eternal laws.

(98-100)

Wordsworth says that man has not only to learn from the living beings but also from Nature.

All creatures and all objects, in degree,

Are friends and patrons of humanity,

There are to whom the garden, grove, and field.

Perpetual lessons of forbearance yield.

(102-106)

In the above discussion of Wordsworth's shorter poems that also included sonnets, odes and some poems which were rather long, it has been seen that Wordsworth's humanism as discussed in the previous chapters is not different from his humanism in this chapter. Jacobus has suggested that the episode of Annette Vallon in Wordsworth's life has some bearing in his writing about the imaginary or real deserted women. Wordsworth also displays his rejection of rationalism and logic. The poet's repertoire of poems is very big therefore only handful of poems were discussed in this chapter.

Works Cited

Alisson, Alexander and Barrow, Eds. The Norton Anthology of Poetry. New York: W.W. Norton Corp. Ltd., 1983.

Haveley, Cecily. Wordsworth The Age of Revolutions Units 13-14 Arts: A Second Level Course. Milton Keynes: The Open University Press, 1976.

Hutchinson, Thomas ed. Poetical Works of Wordsworth. London: Oxford University Press, 1953.

Jacobus, Mary. Tradition and Experiment in the Lyrical Ballads, *1798.* London: Clarendon Press, 1976.

Vincent, Patrick. Review of Toby R. Benis's Romanticism on the Road: The Marginal Gains of Wordsworth's Homeless. New York: St Martin's Press, 2000. Online. <http:// users.ox.ac.uk/ ~scat0385/ 22benis.html>. 31 May 2004.)

6

Humanism in the Prelude

The Prelude (hereinafter, the PL) is perhaps one of the greatest poems by Wordsworth, which he had started in 1797-99 and finished in 1805. It was posthumously published in 1850 and the title was given by Wordsworth's Wife, Mary Hutchinson. Wordsworth had planned the PL as a Prelude to his magnum-opus The Recluse which he never finished. The PL is dedicated to his friend Coleridge, from whom he was estranged in 1807, and even though they reconciled later they could never revive that old camaraderie.

The PL is subtitled a 'Growth of a Poet's Mind'. The Prelude is a long poem consisting of fourteen books tracing the poet's childhood, school and university days to his love of Nature, the influence of the French Revolution and its disappointments and how the poet's imagination was restored. Harvey and Gravil write: "The Prelude is the story of the humanising of the imagination, and a record of how the mature mind, under the guidance of Nature's self, is liberated from nature". (22) Hartman refers to the incidents of Simplon and Snowdon of the poem and say, "It establishes the theme of the poem more clearly than before as a humanist dynamic". (25)

The first book is titled "Introduction Childhood and School-Time" when the young poet experienced joy in all his boyish activities, and felt a sprit of freedom and a sense of independence. The poem opens on an obviously humanistic note, when the poet describes himself as:

A discontented sojourner; now free,

Free as a bird to settle where I will.

(8-9)

The phrase "discontented sojourner" suggests dissatisfaction with the bonds of the present and the desire for freedom, which were the characteristics of the Renaissance humanism.

Wordsworth describes how the Europeans have safeguarded their freedom and independence, alluding to the Frenchman Dominique de Gourgus, who in 1567 "sailed to Florida to avenge the massacre of the French by the Spaniards" (497) and who :

Suffered in silence for Truth's sake; or tell,

How that one Frenchman, through continued force.

Of meditation on the inhuman deeds of those

Who conquered first the Indian Isles.

(205-208)

Indeed, people left their country for the sake of liberty and freedom:

To people the steep rocks and river banks,

Her natural sanctuaries, with a local soul

Of independence and stern liberty.

(218-220)

The word "stern" (220) underlines Wordsworth's belief that liberty is a moral duty.

For Wordsworth, in the humanist tradition truth would be his beacon light:

My last and favourite aspiration, mounts

With yearning toward some philosophic song

Of Truth that cherishes our daily life. (228-230)

In the second book titled "School Time Continued", the poet recollects the good times he had had in those days.

These experiences have produced :

A quiet independence of the heart.....

Fearless of blame, that hence for future days

Ensued a diffidence and modesty.

(72-75)

It was at this time that the poet began to love the sky, the sun, the mountains, the rivers and other aspects of Nature.

This enabled the young boy to learn about life:

Many are our joys

In youth but oh! what happiness to life

When every hour brings palpable access

O knowledge, when all knowledge is delight,

And sorrow is not there!

(283-288)

As in the humanist tradition, Wordsworth's focus throughout the PL is on knowledge, how it is achieved and what it gives to the speaker. The joys of Nature to Wordsworth were the first seeds of creativity, and the creative imagination is a mark of the Renaissance humanism.

In the third book titled "Residence at Cambridge", Wordsworth describes his two year stint at the University which he neglected amidst natural surroundings and his old companions. He writes :

I am not heartless, for there's not a man

That lives who hath not known his god-like hours,

And feels not what an empire we inherit

As natural beings in the strength of Nature.

(190-193)

His distaste for mere academic knowledge is a humanistic:

That way I learned by nature; for my heart
Was social, and loved idleness and joy.

(232-233)

He adds :

Before antiquity and steadfast truth
And strong book-mindedness; and over all
A healthy sound simplicity should reign
A seemly plainness, name it what you will,
Republican or pious.

(393-398)

These ideas are characteristic of both the Renaissance and the Enlightenment humanism.

Book Four, "Summer Vacation", describes the poet's summer holidays. Wordsworth found at this time a "freshness"

In human Life, The daily life of those
Whose occupations really I loved;
The peaceful scene oft filled me with surprise.

(192-194)

Wordsworth concludes this book with a humanitarian description of a soldier for whom he helps find a refuge.

Book Fifth of the PL titled "Books" is also, humanistic, in Wordsworth's dislike for bookish knowledge as seen in his response to Cervantes' novel *Don Quixote*. The poet is grateful for such writers as Shakespeare and Milton, who have enthralled the English for centuries, and for to the classic *Arabian Nights*. He is equally grateful to his kind and loving mother who gave him his first lessons:

> ... she who was the heart
>
> And hinge of all our learnings and our loves;
>
> (257-258)

Wordsworth writes about a boy (whose story is separately included in a poem titled "There was a Boy") died when he was removed from his comrades. This leads the poet to speculate about a child.:

> A race of real children not too wise,
>
> Too learned, or too good, but wanton, fresh,
>
> And bandied up and down by love and hate;
>
> Not unresentful where self-justified;
>
> Fierce, moody, patient, venturous, modest, shy;
>
> Mad at their sports like withered leaves in winds;
>
> Though doing wrong and suffering, and full oft
>
> Bending beneath our life's mysterious weight
>
> Of pain, and doubt, and fear, yet yielding not
>
> In happiness to the happiest upon earth

Simplicity in habit, truth in speech,

Be these the daily strengtheners of their minds;

May books and Nature be their early joy!.

(408-423)

The above extract is humanistic in its praise of those virtues, which are also those of the Renaissance humanism.

In Book Six, titled "Cambridge and the Alps", Wordsworth describes how in the summer vacations of the university he and his sister Dorothy used to go on walking tours with their friends.

There was no joy greater to him than that which he got from his sister's company. He writes :

But thou art with us, with us in the past,

The present, with us in the times to come.

(242-243)

He writes on the power of love, that they share:

There is no grief, no sorrow, no despair,

No languor, no dejection, no dismay,

No absence scarcely can there be for those

Who love as we do!

(244-247)

The poet advocates humane virtues in the following tribute to Coleridge:

For whom it registers the birth, and marks the growth,

Of gentleness, simplicity, and truth,

And joyous loves, that hallow innocent days

Of peace and self-command. Of rivers, fields,

And groves I speak to thee, my Friend! to thee.

(261-265)

In his tour of the Alps the poet was accompanied by a classmate from his university.

He rejoiced in the idea of liberty then, which is one of the characteristics of Renaissance humanism :

Glory and hope to new-born Liberty!

Hail to the mighty projects of the time!

(442-443)

The following lines show the importance of social equality to Wordsworth:

For penitential tears and trembling hopes

Exchanged to equalise in God's pure sight

Monarch and peasant; be the house redeemed.

(454-456)

He also stresses the importance of Nature :

With such a book

Before our eyes, we could not chose but read

Lessons of genuine brotherhood, the plain

And universal reason of mankind.

(543-546)

The above extract highlights importance of both Nature and Brotherhood as seen in the Renaissance humanism.

Book Seven, "Residence in London" is about Wordsworth's experiences in the great city. His first apprehensions of the big city are of awe and wonder at the mass of a variegated humanity:

Now homeward through the thickening hubbub, where:

See, among less distinguishable shapes,

The begging scavenger, with hat in hand;

The Italian, as he treads his way with care,

Steadying, far-seen, a frame of images

Upon his head; with basket at his breast

The Jew; the stately and slow-moving Turk,

With freight of slippers piled beneath his arm!

Enough;—the mighty concourse I surveyed

With no unthinking mind, well pleased to note
Among the crowd all specimens of man,
Through all the colours which the sun bestows,
And every character of form the genial south,
The Frenchman and the Spaniard; from remote
America, the Hunter-India; Moors,
Malays, Lascars, the Tartar, the Chinese,
And Negro Ladies in white muslin gowns.
At leisure, then, I viewed, from day to day,
The spectacles within doors,—birds and beasts
Of every nature, and strange plants convened
From every clime; and , next, those sights that ape

(211-32)

The poet roams about the city as an "idler", suggesting the inquisitiveness of the Renaissance humanism

His humanitarian feeling are revealed when he refers to the Maid of Buttermere and a blind a beggar, the latter despite her pitiable predicament is happy and peaceful along with her child.

He remembers how, as he tells Coleridge :

Those ingenuous moments of our youth

Er we have learnt by use to slight the crimes,

And sorrows of the world.

(331-333)

The poet praises Burke, even though with whom he disagreed and was at logger heads about the French Revolution. He asserts that he would always adhere to the humane qualities of :

courage, or integrity or truth,

Or tenderness, which there set off by foil

Appeared more touching.

(600-602)

In the eighth book "Retrospect - Love of Nature Leading to Love of Man", Wordsworth reiterates his belief that the love of Nature led him to the love of man, and that there is a unity of man and Nature.

The memory of the beautiful landscape of his country home is to Wordsworth more beautiful than the "paradise of ten thousand trees, Gehol's matchless gardens, [of the city] for delight" (77)

George writes, Wordsworth:

Set out to redefine Nature's law not by looking at natural phenomena with the eye of a scientist, nor by looking at the conduct of men and nations with the eye of a political theorist, but by looking with the moralist's eye at the relations between men and their surroundings. He looked most closely of all at the person he knew best:

himself. He had been reared in the country, in surroundings that were natural in the sense that they were hardly altered by any art or industry. Looking back on his childhood from his late twenties onwards, he concluded that his early years had made him a poet, and that even if other men were not made poets, the beauty of the natural world must be a benevolent influence on their character. So nature (the natural world) influences our nature (human behaviour)(37).

The poet accordingly considers a shepherd to be :

Man free, man working for himself, with choice

Of time, and place, and object; by his wants,

His comforts, native occupations, cares,

Cheerfully led to individual ends

Or social and still followed by a train

Unwooed, unthought-of even-simplicity,

And beauty, and inevitable grace.

(104-110)

They belong to the "Tradition of the golden age" (132) for him the shepherd is :

A freeman wedded to his life of hope

And hazard, and here labour interchanged

With that majestic indolence so dear

To native man. A rambling schoolboy, thus

I felt his presence in his own domain,

As of a lord and monster, of a power,

Or genius, under Nature, under God,

Presiding; and severest solitude.

(253-260)

Wordsworth also acknowledges the contribution of his friends to his love of humanity:

Insensibly, each with the other's help.

when my affections first were led

From kindred, friends, and playmates, to partake

Love for the human creature's absolute self,

The noticeable kindliness of heart

Sprang out of fountains, there abounding most,

Where sovereign Nature dictated the tasks.

(120-126)

The poet tells Coleridge that by the time he was twenty-two he had developed the love of man to its fullest. He also tells Coleridge about the source of knowledge :

With strong sensations teeming as it did,

Of past and present, such a place must needs

Have pleased me, seeking knowledge at that time

Fearless than craving power; yet knowledge came,

Sought or unsought, and influxes of power.

(597-605)

Thus Wordsworth regards the senses as the source of knowledge and not the mind, a characteristic of the Enlightenment humanism of Rousseau.

At the end of Book Eight, Wordsworth gives a unified picture of man :

O'er the blue firmament a radiant white,

Descending slow with something heavenly fraught.

Add also that among the multitudes

Of that huge city, oftentimes was seen

Affectingly set forth, more than elsewhere

Is possible, the unity of man.

(662-667)

George writes:

Nature had been his guide to the idea of the unity of man, and the fatherhood of God, and had developed in him love of his race; yet he often sought in her rest and refuge from the lawlessness and guilt of mankind. (306)

Wordsworth concludes Book Eight with a address to Coleridge reflecting on his growth of love for man :

Thus from a very early age, O Friend!

My thoughts by slow gradations had been drawn
To human-kind and to the good and ill
Of human life : Nature had led me on;
And oft amid the busy hum I seemed
To travel independent of her help,
As if I had forgotten her; but no,
The world of human-kind outweighed not hers
In my habitual thoughts; the scale of life,
Though filling daily, still was light, compared
With that in which her mighty objects lay.

(676-686)

Wordsworth discussed his stay in France from the book ninth to the book eleventh of the PL. In "Residence in France" he describes his stay in France during the height of the French Revolution, and his meeting with Michel Beaupuy, who inculcated in him revolutionary and republican ideals, and introduced him to the philosophy of Rousseau and Godwin.

The revolutionaries emphasised :

The faculties of man, receive
Gladly the highest promises, and hail,
As best, the government of equal rights
And individual worth.

(240-243)

About Beaupuy, Wordsworth tells Coleridge that :

We added dearest themes
Man and his noble nature, as it is
The gift which God has placed within his power,
His blind desires and steady faculties
Capable of clear truth, the one to break
Bondage, the other to build liberty
On firm foundations, making social life,
Through knowledge spreading and imperishable,
As just in regulation, and as pure
As individual in the wise and good.

(354-363)

Wordsworth saw that even the meanest man was filled with the zeal of the revolution:

.... Elate we looked
Upon their virtues saw, in rudest men,
Self-sacrifice the firmest; generous love,
And continence of mind, and sense of right,
Uppermost in the midst of fiercest strife.

(385-389)

Beaupuy at the end of his military career became a General and died for the cause of liberty Wordsworth concludes about him that he was :

...most blessed

In this that he the fate of later times

Lived not to see, nor what we now behold,

Who have as ardent hearts as he had then.

(427-430)

At the end of the ninth book Wordsworth shows his scorn for the absolute Monarchy. He also shows his compassion for the poor and the oppressed :

Mixed with pity too

And love, for where hope is there love will be

For the abject multitude. And when we chanced.

(507-509)

Wordsworth believes that the revolutionary is committed to human welfare :

To animate the mind that ever turned

A thought to human welfare —that, henceforth

Captivity by mandate without law.

(534-536)

In the tenth book titled "Residence in France continued" Wordsworth describes the bloodshed of the Reign of Terror, and about Robespierre:

Tis true, had gone before this hour, dire work

Of massacre, in which the senseless sword

Was prayed to as a judge; but these were past

Earth free from them for ever, as was thought,—

Ephemeral monsters, to be seen but once!

Things that could only show themselves and die.

(42-47)

The poet is unhappy with those who had belied the humanistic ideals of the French Revolution by curtailing the freedom of the French people. Wordsworth writes :

Who in attack or in defence were strong

Through their impiety my inmost soul

Was agitated; yea, I could almost

Have prayed that throughout earth upon all men

By patient exercise of reason made

Worthy of liberty, all spirits filled

With zeal expanding in Truth's holy light,

(132-138)

Even though poet was disappointed with the events that took place after the after math of the French Revolution, he did not lose faith in the ideals of the Republic. He believed :

That nothing hath a natural right to last

But equity and reason; that all else

(205-206)

He was so disillusioned with the killings that he feels that he:

Should to the breast of Nature have gone back,

with all my resolutions, all my hopes,

A poet only to myself, to men.

(232-234)

The poet came back to England and to his disappointment found that his country was in war with France. Wordsworth was elated when Robespierre was killed :

Great was my transport, deep my gratitude

To everlasting Justice, be this fiat

Made manifest, Come now, ye golden times

Said I forth-pouring on those open sands

A hymn of triumph: as the morning comes.

(576-580)

Even though France was red with blood, Wordsworth continued to support republican ideas. He concludes the tenth book of the PL by writing about the French people :

Their madness stands declared and visible;

Elsewhere will safety now be sought, and earth

March firmly towards righteousness and peace;

(587-589)

In the eleventh book "France concluded" Wordsworth concludes his experiences and observations about France. Once again Wordsworth reiterates that the evil and wrongful acts of the republican French government would not deter him from his belief in the revolutionary and republican ideals. His trust in people is unshakable. He cautions the French people that the death of one Robespierre could lead to the rule of another one, so the French people should try to safeguard their newly founded republic. In England his humanity overcomes his patriotism and he supports the French Republic, raising his voice against such politicians as Pitt and Burke. He writes :

To daunt me; in the People was my trust,

And in the virtues which mine eyes had seen.

(11-12)

He knows that:

wound external could not take

Life from the young Republic; (13-14)

Wordsworth writes that till the end of his life he would have fought for the humanistic principles of the French Revolution :

And would have fought, even to the death to attest

The quality of the metal which I saw,

What there is best in individual man,

Of wise in passion, and sublime in power,

Benevolent in small societies,

And great in large ones, I had oft revolved. (80-85)

The poet writes that ultimately, it is the laws of the state that are responsible for the misery poverty and wealth of the state for him, after all these years, remembering the past is:

O pleasant exercise of hope and joy

For mighty were the auxiliars which then stood

Upon our side, us who were strong in love!

Bliss was it in that dawn to be alive,

But to be young was very Heaven !

(104-108)

Wordsworth further writes that the British law makers had to make laws for the welfare of the people not some where in any utopia but in England itself :

... in the very world, which is the world

Of all of us,— the place where, in the end,

We find our happiness, or not at all!

(142-144)

Legouis writes :

Wordsworth saw his native country prepare fleets and armies to attack the nation which in his eyes represented progress. Which of the two sentiments, patriotism or the love of humanity, was to obtain the mastery within him. It was patriotism, in this painful struggle, that had to accept defeat. (232)

Wordsworth realized that the French, who had revolted against the oppression of the rulers, had themselves became the oppressors.

George comments:

In this act his last hopes of liberty suffered eclipse, and he was overwhelmed with shame and despondency; yet his hatred of oppression became stronger than ever, for he believed that in this movement all the darkest events of the old regime were combined. (314)

This was his moral crisis. In these times he was supported by his sister and his friend Coleridge.

In the twelfth book, "Imagination and Taste, How Impaired And Restored", Wordsworth writes about the normalization process after the disappointments with the French Revolution. He had gone into a moral crisis after the bloody events.

The opening lines of the book show Wordsworth's reaction against the human suffering :

Long time have human ignorance and guilt,

Detained us, on what spectacles of woe

Compelled to look, and inwardly oppressed

With sorrow, disappointment, vexing thoughts,.....

(1-4)

He once again writes about the power of Nature to influence man :

ye breezes and soft airs,

Whose subtle intercourse with breathing flowers,

Feelingly watched, might teach man's haughty race

How without injury to take, to give

Without offence; ye who, as if to show

The wondrous influence of power gently used ....

(9-14)

Wordsworth tells Coleridge that in this book of the PL and in the next he wants to write about "intellectual power and fostering love." (45).

The poet believes that poets :

they will speak to thee

More perfectly of purer creatures;

(68-9)

The above extract is imbued with the ideas of humanism in its advocacy of poetry for the betterment o the human beings. To quote George again :

He [Wordsworth] transferred his observation and analysis now from Man to Nature, and put her under the malignant spell, and the result was the denuding and unsouling of all natural scenes and objects. Nature became a laboratory instead of a garden. (319)

Wordsworth believed that the sensual eye almost acted in a tyrannical:

When the bodily eye, in every stage of life
The most despotic of our senses, gained
Such strength in me as often held my mind
In absolute dominion. Gladly here,
Entering upon abstruser argument,
Could I endeavour to unfold the means
Which Nature studiously employs to thwart
This tyranny, summons all the senses each
To counteract the other, and themselves,
Are makes them all, and the object with which all
Are conversant, subservient in their turn
To the great ends of Liberty and power.
But leave we this; enough that my delights
(Such as they were) were sought insatiably,
Vivid the transport, vivid though not profound.

(128-140)

The above extract reflects the influence of the philosophical ideas of the eighteenth century.

Wordsworth further writes about his meeting and with Mary Hutchinson who later became his wife.

His communion with Nature made him decide to he a poet:

> I had known
> Too forcibly, too early in my life,
> Visitings of imaginative power
> For this to last: I shook the habit off
> Entirely and for ever, and again
> In Nature's presence stood, as now I stand,
> A sensitive being, a creative soul.
>
> (201-7)

Nature instilled in him a virtue that in times of distress and disappointment he could slight these things.

Wordsworth concludes the book with a description of the two incidents from his childhood whose memory gave him much strength in his later life. The first was when he was not even six years old, and he and a girl carrying a pitcher on her head. Wordsworth writes :

> .... It was, in truth,
> An ordinary sight; but I should need
> Colours and words that are unknown to man,
> To paint the visionary dreariness....
>
> (253-56)

The poet writes :

And think ye not with radiance more sublime
For these remembrances, and for the power
They had left behind? So feeling comes in aid
Attends us, if but once we have been strong.

(268-71)

In another incident of his childhood, the poet remembers a blasted hawthorn tree.

These two incidents left a lasting impression on his life:

That day so lately past, when from the crag
I looked in such anxiety of hope;
With trite reflections of morality,
Yet in the deepest passion, I bowed low
To God, Who thus corrected my desires.

(312-16)

Book Thirteenth, "Imagination", contains his thoughts on the restoration of his imagination after it received a set back following the Reign of Terror.

He pays tribute to Nature, saying that it gives emotion and calmness to the human mind :

That energy by which he seeks the truth,

From her that happy stillness of the mind

Which fits him to receive it when unsought.

(7-10)

George writes :

Returning now from the study of Science to the beauty and sublimely of Nature, he found in her the "image of right reason", which he could take with him into the world of man. (318)

Wordsworth writes that the gratitude and the confidence in truth enables him to pour out the words smoothly and effortlessly :

Smooth task! for words find easy way, inspired

By gratitude, and confidence in truth

It is noteworthy that gratitude and truth were the qualities of the Renaissance humanism.

(14-15)

He looks for human subjects for his poetry :

Long time in search of knowledge did I range

The field of human life, in heart and mind....

(16-17)

Wordsworth now focuses on man :

Whate'er there is desirable and good

Of kindred permanence, unchanged in form

And function, of, through strict vicissitude

Of life and death,

(35-38)

He writes that from the beginning of his childhood he had trained himself to look about man and living creatures:

From moral purpose-early tutored me

To look with feelings of fraternal love

Upon the unassuming things that hold

A silent station in this beauteous world.

(44-47)

Thus he found in man :

object of delight,

Of pure imagination, and of love.

(49-50)

To quote George again:

His emotion being now under regulation, he determined to find out the truths of human life, and what were the elements of permanence in human feelings. He gave up his sanguine schemes for the regeneration of mankind, and turned to the abodes of simple men, where duty, love, and reverence were to be found in their true relation and worth. Here he found that human heart, the haunt and main region of song.

(318)

With the tool of human understanding and the intellect Wordsworth probes further into truths regarding human life:

And, as the horizon of my mind enlarged,
Again I took the intellectual eye
For my instructor, studious more to see
Great truths, than touch and handle little ones.
Knowledge was given accordingly; my trust
Became more firm in feelings that had stood
The lest of such a trial; clearer far
My sense of excellence of right and wrong;
The promise of the present time retired
Into its true proportion; sanguine schemes,
Ambitious projects, pleased me less; I sought
For present good in life's familiar face,
And built thereon my hopes of good to come.

(51-63)

Wordsworth says that it is a weakness of people that they are ruled by others :

Presumption, folly, madness, in the men
Who thrust themselves upon the passive world
As Rulers of the world; to see in these,

Even when the public welfare is their arm,....

(66-69)

The poet looks further for the causes of human miseries and sorrows. He could not understand about the problems of common man by sitting in the cities such as London; and turned towards Nature:

Therefore did I turn
To you, ye pathways, and ye lonely roads;
Sought you enriched with everything I prized,
With human kindness and simple joys.

(116-119)

Meditation in peace and calmness leads Wordsworth to wisdom about human nature:

Was that of wandering on from day to day
Where I could meditate in peace, and cull
Knowledge that step by step might lead me
To wisdom; or as lightsome as a bird
Wafted upon the wind from distant lands,
Sing notes of greeting to strange fields or groves,
Which lacked not voice to welcome me in turn;
And, when that pleasant toil had ceased to lease,
Converse with men, where if we meet a face

We almost meet a friend, on naked heaths

With long long ways before, by cottage bench,

Or well-spring where the weary traveller rests.

(130-141)

Again, George writes: "His wounded heart was healed as he experienced the "love in huts where poor men lie"." (318)

Initially Wordsworth did not speak to the persons he met on the streets, but later he talked to them in order to gain an insight into their lives :

To watch and question those I met, and speak

Without reserve to them, the lonely roads

Were open schools in which I daily read

With most delight the passions of mankind,

There saw into the depth of human souls,

Souls that appear to have no depth at all

To careless eyes. And-now convinced at heart

(161-168)

Talking to them made him realize how much there was in their lives and their stories that were so far ignored, and this made him turn even more to common people for the material of his poetry.

Wordsworth writes that formal education does not teach a "With real feeling and just sense" (172) In fact, love cannot exist amidst the artificialities of social life:

... there indeed,

Love cannot be; nor does it thrive with ease

Among there close and overcrowded haunts

Of cities, where the human heart is sick,

And the eye feeds it not, and cannot feed.....

(196-205)

The poet thinks that the world is misled above all, by bookish knowledge:

How we mislead each other; above all,

How books misled us, seeking their reward

From judgments of the wealthy Few, who see

By artificial lights; how they debase

The Many for the pleasure of those Few;

Effeminately level down the truth

To certain general notions, for the sake

Of being understood at once, or else

Through want of better knowledge in the heads

That frame them; flattering self-conceit with words,

That, while they most ambitiously set forth

Extrinsic differences, the outward marks

Whereby society has parted man
From man, neglect the universal heart.

(207-219)

This is of course an attack on Augustan social and intellectual norms. Further Wordsworth pays tribute to the human mind:

Of these, said I, shall be my song; of these,
If future years mature me for the task,
Will record the praises, making verse
Deal boldly with substantial things; in truth
And sanctity of passion, speak of these,
That justice may be done, obeisance paid
Where it is due: thus haply shall I teach,
Inspire; through unadulterated ears
Pour rapture, tenderness, and hope,-my theme
No other than the very heart of man,
As found among the best of those who live-
Not unexalted by religious faith,
Nor uninformed by books, good books

(227-244)

Wordsworth also shows his sympathy for:

Meek men, whose very souls perhaps would sink
Beneath them, summoned to such intercourse;
Theirs is the language of the heavens, the power,
The thought, the image, and the silent joy;
Words are but under-agents in their souls;
When they are grasping with their greatest strength,

(269-273)

In Book Fourteenth Wordsworth presents a grand picture of the poet as a teacher. He writes in the book about the qualities of love and freedom, pays tributes to his sister, his wife and his friends, and acknowledges the role of Nature in shaping his humanity. The poet writes that one should not be crushed under the weight of problems and troubles of daily life but, rather, should remain calm and unperturbed. He meditates on love, which removes fear. Love may be found in flowers and animals too :

....The lamb
And the lamb's mother, and their tender ways
Shall touch thee to the heart; thou callest this love,
And not inaptly so, for love it is,
Far as it carries thee. In some green bower
Rest,...

(173-177)

The higher form of love frees a soul from the chains of the body :

Impassioned, but delight how pitiable !

Unless this love by a still higher love

Be hallowed, love that breathes not without awe;

Love that adores, but on the knees of prayer,

By heaven inspired; that frees from chains the soul,....

(181-85)

It the progress of civilization :

The works of man and face of human life;

And lastly from its progress have we drawn

Faith in life endless the sustaining thought

Of human Being, Eternity, and God,....

In the last two above quoted extracts which are only some among many one sees Wordsworth's love for animals and trees. It shows his concern not only for the animals but also for plants or the environment in general. "In some green bower" (177).

It is noteworthy the twentieth century Wordsworth's poetry came under the microscopic scrutiny of Ecocritism.

(202-205)

As well as friendship and romance, because it has the power to complete perfect a man :

Oh, joy to him who here hath sown, hath laid
Here the foundation of his future years !
For all that friendship, all that love can do,
All that a darling countenance can look
Or dear voice utter, to complete the man,
Perfect him,....

(218-23)

Love makes a man humble and tender :

... his heart
Be tender as a nursing mother's heart;
Of female softness shall his life be full,
Of humble cares and delicate desires,
Mild interests and gentlest sympathies.

(226-230)

He once again pays tribute to Dorothy and his wife:

Shall I be silent ? O capacious Soul !...
Shall I be mute, are thou be spoken of ?
Thy kindred influence to my heart of hearts
did also find its way,...

(277-82)

Wordsworth concludes the poem with a humanistic reiteration of his commitment to humanity :

Anon I rose

Vast prospect of the world which I had been

And was; and hence this Song, which like a lark

I have protracted, in the unwearied heavens

Singing, and often with more plaintive voice

To earth attempered and her deep-drawn sighs,

Yet centring all in love, and in the end

All gratulant, if rightly understood.

(379-87)

If rightly Even if he and his fellow-poets (epitomized by Coleridge) die and the world return to its old "idolatry" (434) and "servitude" (435), to "ignominy and shame" (436):

...we shall still

Find solace—knowing what we have learnt to know,

Rich in true happiness if allowed to be

Faithful alike in forwarding a day

Of firmer trust, joint labourers in the work

(Should Providence such grace to us vouchsafe)

Of their deliverance, surely yet to come.

Prophets of Nature, we to them will speak

A lasting inspiration sanctified
Be reason, blest by faith; what we have loved,
Others will love, and we will teach them how;
Instruct them how the mind of man becomes
A thousand times more beautiful than the earth
On which he dwells, above this frame of things
(Which, mid all revolution in the hopes
And rears of man, doth still remain unchanged)
In beauty exalted, as it is itself
Of quality and fabric more divine.

(437-54)

Works Cited

Harvey, W.J. and Richard Gravil, Eds. The Prelude, A Casebook. London: The Macmillan Press Ltd., 1972.

Haveley, Cecily. Wordsworth. The Age of Revolutions, Units 13-14, Arts: A Second Level Course. Milton Keynes: The Open University Press, 1976.

Legouis, Emile. The Early Life of Wordsworth : The Prelude, a Critical Study. London: Oxford University Press, 1932.

Wordsworth, William. The Prelude. ed. A.J. George. London: D.C. Heath & Company, 1930.

Prelude. ed. J.C. Maxwell. Hermondsworth: Penguin Books Ltd., 1972.

Poetical Works of Wordsworth. ed. Thomas Hutchinson. London: Oxford University Press, 1953.

7

Humanism in the Excursion

Wordsworth's another long poem, The "Excursion" (The EC) was published in 1814. It is in nine books. The entire poem is a humanistic exploration of the social, political and educational concerns of the time, and reveal also Wordsworth's humanitarian instincts in the narration of the stories of the Wanderer, the solitary and other characters. He remarks in the Preface of the poem that his intention was "to compose a philosophical poem, containing views of Man, Nature, and Society" (589) and to call it "The Recluse". The EC was planned as the middle portion of the longer work "The Recluse" (The R). The first book, "The Wanderer" was earlier published as "The Ruined Cottage". The poet describes here how he met the Wanderer and asked him about his education and his life. He shows the Wanderer as a person strongly influenced by Nature.

The Wanderer was a herdsman, whose parents had brought up their children in religious and pious atmosphere:

The Wanderer was from the beginning deeply influenced by the power of Nature and its lessons of love :

Or flowing from the universal face
Of earth and sky. But he has felt the power
Of Nature, and already was prepared,
By his intense conceptions, to receive
Deeply the lesson deep of love which he,
Whom Nature, by whatever means, has taught
......
His animal being; in them did he live,
And by them did he live; they were his Life.
......
That made him; it was blessedness and love!

(209-218)

He loved to read the "divine Milton" (250), (Milton was, as mentioned earlier, the humanist who most influenced the Romantics) and his school-master provided him with,

...books that explain
The purer elements of truth involved
In lines and numbers, and, by charm severe,
(Especially perceived where nature droops
And feeling is suppressed) preserve the mind

Busy in solitude a poverty

(252-57)

The Wanderer left home to become a peddler so that he could discover more about life. His experience taught him sympathize with his fellow human being, and now he was a source of strength, because his "religion" (409) was "self taught" (410), inspired by "grace divine" (412), and "human reason dictated with "awe" (413). These are of course humanist ideals.

The Wanderer, says a poet felt the pain of others :

He could afford to suffer

With those whom he saw suffer.

(370-71)

Wordsworth considers himself fortunate that the wanderer took him to be his chosen comrade. The Wanderer told him the story of the last inhabitant of a ruined cottage where was living a widow. Her husband had become a sailor because of poverty and could not take his pregnant wife and his infant along with him on sea. Whenever the Wanderer met Margaret, the widow he saw her in dire poverty. It was only the thought of her two children that stopped her from dying. Then her younger child dies, but Margaret continued to struggle for the sake of her elder son until she herself dies, too. The poet reviews :

... and traced

Fondly though with an interest more mild,

That secret spirit of humanity.

(925-27)

In the second book Titled "The Solitary" the poet meets a friend of the Wanderer, whom he labels 'Solitary'.

The humanism that Wordsworth evinces in this book of the EC is Roussean in nature, for he depicts the Wanderer as a 'natural' man.

Wherever the narrator goes with the Wanderer he finds that the aged traveller was known to all the inhabitants he met on the public ways :

Rich in love

And sweet humanity, he was himself,

To the degree that he desired, beloved.

Smiles of good-will from faces that he knew.

(55-58)

The Wanderer had become a priest for "the cause of Christ and civil liberty" (221) but later, under the influence of the French Revolution, he gave the priesthood, and became a free man :

And every day and every place enjoyed

The unshackled layman's natural liberty;

Speech, manners, morals, all without disguise.

(264-266)

The Wanderer takes the narrator on mountaineering trip. There they hear a mournful song being sung at a funeral Wordsworth feels a bonding with the funeral procession :

(How far soe'er a stranger) does not own

The bond of brotherhood, when he sees them go,

A mute procession on the houseless road;

(561-3)

In a penthouse, amidst children's playthings, he sees a book, Voltaire's novel the Optimist. His companion feels it is his friend's, and that the funeral party must have been for his friend. But soon they see this friend trying to console a child.

Wordsworth describes the simple and humble rustic life of the mountaineers in this part of the EC.

In the third book titled "Despondency" the Solitary, the friend of the Wanderer, tells narrator about himself. He too he had become an ardent supporter of the French Revolution and was disappointed with the aftermath. That is why he had migrated to America. He knows, however, that:

Night hushed as night, and day serene as

—But why this tedious record?—Age, we know,

Is garrulous; and solitude is apt

To anticipate the privilege of Age.

From far ye come; and surely with a hope

Of better entertainment:—let us hence!

Loth to forsake the spot, and still more loth

To be diverted from our present theme,

(324-31).

He dreams of a monastic brotherhood : "An undissolving fellowship" (396), and wonders that what God has given to man:

What good is given to men,

More solid than the gilded clouds of heaven?

What joy more lasting than a vernal flower?

None! 'tis the general plaint of human kind.

(437-440)

The Solitary married a dear and loving woman with whom he had spent many wonderful years, but she died and he became all alone. But :

Society became my glittering bride,

And airy hopes my children.

(735-6)

He allowed himself to be guided by Nature :

The nature of the dissolute; but thee,

O fostering Nature! I rejected smiled

At others' tears in pity; and in scorn

At those, which thy soft influence sometimes drew

From my unguarded heart.—The tranquil shores

(808-12)

The fourth book "Despondency Corrected" gives a philosophical account of the conversations among the three men. They talk about the benefits of Nature, and agree that even the smallest and minute being can offer some knowledge.

In the following lines the poet indicates the importance of the humanistic quality of hope :

Hope, below this, consists not with belief
In mercy, carried infinite degrees
Beyond the tenderness of human hearts;
Hope, below this, consists not with belief
In perfect wisdom, guiding mightiest power,
That finds no limits but her own pure will.

(191-196)

And liberty :

The liberty, for frail, for moral, man
To roam at large among unpeopled glens
And mountainous retirements, only trod
By devious footsteps; regions consecrate
To oldest time! And, reckless of the storm.

(514-518)

The Solitary feels that men :

In framing models to improve the scheme
Of man's existence, and recast the world,
Why should not grave Philosophy be styled,
Herself, a dreamer of a kindred stock.

(336-39)

Must understand human nature and go beyond that to explore all nature to "All natures,—to the end that he may find/The law that governs each" (334-5), because:

For knowledge is delight; and such delight
Breeds love: yet, suited as it rather is
To thought and to the climbing intellect,
It teaches les to love, than to adore;
If that be not indeed the highest love!

(346-50)

The poet also speaks of the knowledge stored in books:

Within whose silent chambers treasure lies
Preserved from age to age; more precious far
Than that accumulated store of gold
And orient gems, which, for a day of need.

(564-568)

In the fifth book titled "The Pastor" the poet writes about a pastor, an old acquaintance of the Solitary, about his church and the churchyard. Wordsworth says that Christian civilization has instilled the virtues of justice and freedom. Besides, looking at the pastor, he feels that:

— Knowledge, methinks, in these disordered times,

Should be allowed a privilege to have

Her anchorites, like piety of old;

Men, who, from faction sacred.

(29-32)

The Solitary describes a big house which was a symbol of feudalism which he contrasts with the pastor.

A rural lord might dwell No feudal pomp,

Or power, replied the Wanderer, to that House

Belongs, but there in his allotted Home

Abides, from year to year, a genuine Priest,

The shepherd of his flock; or, as a king

Is styled, when most affectionately praised,

The father of his people.

(97-103)

The Solitary tells the Wanderer and the narrator that the pastor has been a good religious instructor to the simple folk of the mountains and has taken good care of his flock, providing them with:

The clearest apprehension of those truths,

Which unassisted reason's utmost power.

(520-521)

The narrator says that loneliness or solitude can lead to humanity but not to cruelty or vice. Humanity is called "motherly" (926) by Wordsworth

The poet concludes the fifth book of the EC with the following passage that is filled with the spirit of the Renaissance humanism :

The faith partaking of those holy times,

Life, I repeat, is energy of love

Divine or human; exercised in pain,

In strife, in tribulation; and ordained,

If so approved and sanctified, to pass,

Through shades and silent rest, to endless joy.

(1011-1016)

The sixth and seventh books titled "The Churchyard Among the Mountains" describe in humanitarian fashion the people in their graves. Hutchinson writes that an Epitaph, "should speak in a tone which shall sink into the heart, the general language of humanity..." (731)

Men, whose delight is where their duty leads

Or fixes them; whose least distinguished day.

(47-49)

The pastor tells his audience about a physician who had cured a person who become deranged after receiving a set-back in love by asking him to present his beloved a book. The patient henceforth became a great lover of books : "Resolved to quell his pain, and search for truth" (152)

Ellen, is a bubbly and sprightly girl who enjoys herself thoroughly in her simple and rural surroundings. She becomes an unwed mother, and later leaves her mother and her infant to seek her livelihood as a foster mother. The parents of the foster-child never allows her to visit her own infant not even to attend its funeral. But Ellen refuses to obey them and in the end leaves them. Another man leaves his dear wife and child to seek life else were, yet another has six worthy daughters who take control of the household after their mother's death. Through all these stories emerge the picture of struggling and sorrowful humanity.

In the seventh book, the pastor continues with the stories of the dead people. The poet describes the family of the pastor as well as another clergyman, who is also devoted to his profession.

The clergyman is kind towards the poor, who loves him, he is also devoted towards his profession.

The poet concludes the seventh book with a description about the chivalry of the British soldiers :

When joy of war and pride of chivalry

Languished beneath accumulated years,

Had power to draw him from the world.

(936-938)

In Book Eight, "The Parsonage", the poet describes the parsonage and the household of the parson. The poet stresses the importance of the wisdom of the old:

The sober sympathies of long-tried friends.

By these Itinerants, as experienced men,

Counsel is given; contention they appease

With gentle language; in remotest wilds,

Tears wipe away, and pleasant tidings bring.

(76-80)

The parson himself extols the virtues of the England :

...the blessed Isle,

Truth's consecrated residence, the seat

Impregnable of Liberty and Peace.

(145-147)

The family of the parson is pious and religious. The poet hopes that by "learning" (214) the people all over the world would make their nations prosperous :

Of this dominion over nature gained,

Men of all lands shall exercise the same

In due proportion to their country's need;

Learning, though late, that all true glory rests.

(211-214)

The poet also hopes that the British would try to preserve their customs and traditions that reflect piety :

Sadness and keen regret, we who revere.
And would preserve as things above all price,
The old domestic morals of the land,
Her simple manners, and the stable worth
That dignified and cheered a low estate?
Oh! where is now the character of peace,
Sobriety, and order, and chaste love.

(234-240)

The life of the countryside is characterized by:

... honest dealing, and untainted speech,
And pure good-will, and hospitable cheer;

(241-42)

Wordsworth says that in the present times when the English moral and religious life has deteriorated, English schools are trying to inculcate the old values in young boys and girls :

Performs its functions; rarely competent,
To impress a vivid feeling on the mind
If what there is delightful in the breeze,
The gentle visitations of the sun,

Or lapse of liquid element by hand,

Or foot, or lip, in summer's warmth perceived.

Can hope look forward to a manhood raised

On such foundations?

(327-334)

In the ninth book "Discourse of the Wanderer, and An Evening Visit to the Lake", Wordsworth continues with the description of the parson's home. They indulge in a philosophical conversation; among other topics they discuss the character of the English people, the virtue of labour and the soul of man. The Wanderer is confident that the British with their vigour and energy would triumph.

This reveals Wordsworth's belief in Renaissance's humanistic qualities of hope and action, of liberty and of knowledge.

When the Person talks about his hopes, his words suggest the virtues of the Renaissance humanism.

This Land shall witness; and as days roll on,

Earth's universal frame shall feel the effect;

Even till the smallest habitable rock,

Beaten by lonely billows, hear the songs

Of humanised society; and bloom

With civil arts, that shall breath forth their fragrance...

On Albion's noble Race in freedom born.

Expect these mighty issues: from the pains.

(387-393)

England is "The happy Island where ye think and act;" (412)

The poem ends thus on a note of hope, a marker of Wordsworth's humanism.

As has been seen in the earlier chapters Wordsworth's major poetry then comprising of the Lyrical Ballads, shorter poems of the anthologies of 1805, 1807, 1815, 1819, 1822 and the longer poems such as the Prelude and the Excursion is perforated not only with his humanitarianism but also with philosophical humanisms of the Renaissance and the Enlightenment.

It has been observed that, humanism is also present in the English poetry from Chaucer to the Romantics; some poets display only humanitarianism in their works such as William Langland, Geoffrey Chaucer, and Pre Romantics like James Thomson, Thomas Gray, Oliver Goldsmith, George Crabbe and Robert Burns, while, some poets display either Renaissance or Enlightenment humanism in their poetry like Edmund Spenser, William Shakespeare John Milton, John Donne and Alexander Pope. No other poet than Wordsworth has blended in his poetry humanitarianism with the philosophical humanism.

It can be said that Wordsworth's humanism transcends humanity; that is, it does not confine itself only to humans but extends to all the animate world. Wordsworth as a child was an extremely sensitive boy. It is said that at the age of eight he cried when he saw for the first time trees being cut.

His poetry seems to echo Coleridge's well-known lines from the "Ancient Mariner" :

> He prayeth best who loveth best,
>
> All things both great and small.
>
> (647-648)

Wordsworth major poems may also be called "humanist" according to twentieth century norms as defined in the three Humanist Manifestos.

Willey sums-up the humanistic poetry of Wordsworth:

Many and great changes have taken place since Wordsworth's time, changes which have involved the evaporation of most of his characteristic beliefs, both inherited and self-wrought. Few now have and faith in 'nature'... Yet as he s the first, so he remains the type, of the 'modern' poets who, 'left alone' with a vaster material than his, must bear as best they can, unaided by any universally held mythology, the 'weight of all this unintelligible world' (309). Weats, Eliot and the MacSpauday poets are such 'modern' poets who have had continued humanistic tradition of English poetry though they may not have always been influenced by Wordsworth.

Works Cited

ed. Thomas Hutchinson. Poetical Works of Wordsworth. London: Oxford University Press, 1953.

Willey, Basil. The Eighteenth Century Background. London: Chatau and Windmus, 1957.

8

Post script : Wordsworth as a Bolshevist

The post script, 'Wordsworth as Bolshevist' was not in the original plan of the book, but it came as an after thought after reading Prof. Herbert J.C. Grierson's book Milton and Wordsworth. In the book Grierson has compared bolshevism of Milton and Wordsworth and has observed:

> Milton appears as so bold and individual a thinker, so remote from the Presbyterian, independent or Baptist. But Milton steered right on, however uncharted the seas, a Bolshevist in virtue alike of his intolerant temperament and his confident intellectualism. With Wordsworth it was otherwise...
>
> However far Wordsworth has gone and however obstinately he clung to his democratic tenets and sympathies, his was no Bolshevist temperament. He was no ruthless intellectual, following to its last consequence what the late Lord Salisbury called "the dead-reckoning of logic", nor was his age such an intellectual era as the seventeenth century.

I am afraid, I do not agree with Prof. Grierson's observation. Earlier Grierson had quoted from Wordsworth's letter written to Bishop Richard Watson in 1793, when he came to know that England had attacked republic France, but he did not quote from the letter that part which shows that Wordsworth had acquired bolshevist sensibilities after coming in contact with Michel Beaupuy, the French Soldier who became his revolutionary mentor:

> For liberty is too often obliged "*to borrow the very arms of Despotism in order to overthrow him, and, in order to reign in peace, must establish herself by violence.* (Italics mine) She deplores such stern necessity, but the safety of the people, her supreme law, is her consolation."
>
> (qtd. in Legouis 128)

Who could have written or spoken such lines other than a bolshevist who was angry with the system, inequalities, the corruption, poverty and injustice prevailing in the society. The afore mentioned quotation are quoted in the first chapter of this book prompting me to label Wordsworth as a "Marxist".

Earlier when Wordsworth was disappointed with the September Massacres in 1792 in France, he had expressed his antipathy towards revolution and violence in a letter to his friend Mathew:

> I recoil from the very idea of a revolution. I am a determined enemy to every species of violence. I see no connection, but what the obstinacy of pride and ignorance renders necessary, between justice and the sword between reason and bonds.
>
> (qtd. in Legouis, 248)

Wordsworth's this letter to Mathew as quoted in Legouis is not dated but going by its contents vis-a-vis

Wordsworth's letter to Watson written later implies clearly that Wordsworth had written to Mathew before meeting Beaupuy. When Wordsworth had left for France in 1973, he was not even a republican and it took Beaupuy sometime to convert him into a republican. Once Wordsworth was convinced of the necessity of the revolution and its ideals of equality, fraternity and brotherhood, he became an ardent supporter and worshiper of the revolution approving of violence to bring social changes.

Wordsworth did not join any freedom struggle because there was none in England at that time, like it was done by Byron and Christopher Caldwell who took Guns in their hands instead of Pen when they felt the need to do so and died too like Beaupuy, while fighting for freedom.

The difference between bolshevism of Milton and Wordsworth is that Milton was the avowed spokesperson of the republican views and a known supporter of Cromwell whereas Wordsworth did not find a publisher for his letter written to Watson and did not publish The Prelude in his life time, which he had completed in 1805 and shows his disapproval of the war that was started by Britain and its allies against the republic France in 1793:

> This threw me first out of the pale of love
>
> Soured and corrupted, upwards to the source,
>
> My sentiments; was not, as hitherto,
>
> A swallowing up of lesser things in great,
>
> But change of them into their contraries.
>
> (the PL, xi, 175-180)

Wordsworth's love of republicanism overcomes his patriotism:

What had been a pride,

Was now a shame; my liking and my loves

Ran in new channels, leaving old ones dry;

(the PL, xi,)

Only few of English writers before Wordsworth had criticized the British Monarchy or its policies, famous of them is Milton, followed by Henry Fielding and perhaps Shakespeare too.

Milton was saved by his age and the Restored Monarchy believed that he was too old and also blind to cause any harm to it.

Fielding in his burlesques and satires had ridiculed the British government's policies and consequently they were banned forcing him to novel writing. Thomas Hardy was forced to return to poetry, after the Prudish Victorian society raised hue and cry in the print media over his novel Jude the Obscure.

Shakespeare in his flourishing dramatic career never attacked Queen Elizabeth or her policies and the only time he seemed to do so in one of his last plays, The Tempest, a political allegory criticizing the Queen's imperialist policies it curtailed his career though he wrote some more plays after The Tempest, but they were poor shadows of his more illustrious ones.

When The Prelude was completed in 1805 Wordsworth did not enjoy similar stature to that of Shakespeare and

Milton so as to expect any reprieve from the British society for favouring the enemy to his homeland. Had he published the poem, he might have been charged for treason and moreover he had a wife and an unmarried sister to support. So, in publishing The Prelude in 1805 he had lots of stakes to think of.

It is unfortunate that wordsworth who in his twenty third year was a juggernaut of the ideals of the French revolution in his seventy third year opposed liberal reforms as in ballot. This incongruity in ideas has been attributed to Wordsworth's infirmity of old age. Martin says:

"Often his judgment was at fault from mere failure to gather all the relevant facts, and for this old age was responsible. There was a period of slowly decaying power, and you see it, as Professor Harper has shown, in occasional mistakes of memory contained in the notes of 1843. The cause of this was the very ardour of his lovely sensibilities and right enthusiasms in earlier years" (52), but there is no doubt that Wordsworth's finest poetry was written under the influence, rather spell of the French revolution.

To establish a just and an egalitarian society violent revolutions have to take place as it happened in Nepal because Gorbachows of the world are hard to come by.

Works-cited

Martin, A.D. The Religion of Wordsworth. London George Aleen & Unwin Ltd. 1936

Grierson, Herbert J.C. Milton & Wordsworth: Poets and Prophets. London: Cambridge University Press, 1937.

Hutchinson, Thomas, ed. Poetical Works of Wordsworth. London: Oxford University Press, 1953.

Legouis, Emile. The Early Life of Wordsworth : The Prelude, a Critical Study. New York: P. Dutton & Company, 1932.

Appendix - I

CONTENTS OF THE 1798 EDITION OF THE LYRICAL VALLADS

The Rime of the Ancyent Marinere

The Foster-Mother's Tale

Lines left upon a Seat in a yew-tree which stands near the Lake of Esthwaite

The Nightingale, a Conversational poem

The Female Vagrant

Goody Blake and Harry Gill

Lines written at a small distance from my House, and sent by my Little Boy to the Person to whom they are addressed

Simon lee, the old Huntsman

Anecdote for Fathers

We are seven

Lines written in early spring

The Thorn

The last of the Flock

The Dungeon

The mad Mother

The Idiot Boy

Lines written near Richmond, upon the Thames, at Evening

Expostulation and Reply

The Tables Turned; and Evening Scene, on the same subject

Old Man traveling

The Complaint of a forsaken Indian Women

The Convict

Lines written a few miles above Tintern Abbey

Appendix - II

CONTENTS OF THE 1800 EDITION OF THE LYRICAL VALLADS

Expostulation and Reply

The Tables turned; and Evening scene, on the same subject

Animal Tranquility and Decay, a Sketch

The Complaint of a forsaken Indian Women

The last of the Flock

Lines left upon a Seat in a yew-tree which stands near the Lake of Esthwaite

The Foster-Mother's Tale

Goody Blake and Harry Gill

The Thorn

We are Seven

Anecdote for Fathers

Lines written at a small distance from my House, and sent by me little Boy to the person to whom they are addressed

The Female Vagrant

The Dungeon

Simon Lee, the old Huntsman

Lines written in early Spring

The Nightingale, written in April, 1798

Lines written when sailing in a Boat at Evening

Lines written near Richmond, upon the Thames

The Idiot Boy

Love

The Mad Mother

The Ancient Mariner

Lines written above Tintern Abbey

Hart-leap Well

There was a Boy, & c

The Brothers, a Pastoral poem

Ellen Irwin, or the Braes of Kirtle

Strange fits of passion I have known, & c

Song

A Slumber did my spirit seal, & c

The Waterfall and the Eglantine

The Oak and the Broom, a Pastoral

Lucy Gray

The Idle Shepher-Boys, or Dungeon-Gill Force, a pastoral'Tis said that some have died for love, & c

Poor Susan

Inscription for the Spot where the Hermitage stood on St Herbert's Island, Derwent-Water

Inscription for the House (an Outhouse) on the Island at Grasmere

To a Sexton

Andrew Jones

The Two Thieves, or The last Stage of Avarice

A whirl-blast from behind the Hill

Song for the wandering Jew

Ruth

Lines written with a Slate-Pencil upon a Stone, & c

Lines written on a Tablet in a School

The two April Mornings

The Fountain, a Conversation

Nutting

Three years she grew in sun and shower, & c

The Pet-Lamb, a Pastoral

Written in Germany on one of the Coldest days of the century

The Childless Father

The Old Cumberland Beggar, a Description

Rural Architecture

A Poet's Epitaph

A Character

A Fragment

Poems on the Naming of Places

Michael, a Pastoral

Notes to the Poem of The Brothers

Notes to the Poem of Michael

Appendix - III

ADVERSITEMENT TO LYRICAL BALLADS (1798)

It is the honourable characteristic of Poetry that its materials are to be found in every subject which can interest the human mind. The evidence of this fact is to be sought, not in the writings of Critics, but in those of Poets themselves.

The majority of the following poems are to be considered as experiments. They were written chiefly with a view to ascertain how fat the language of conversation in the middle and lower classes of society is adapted to the purposes of poetic pleasure. Readers accustomed to the gaudiness and inane phraseology of many modern writers, if they persist in reading this book to its conclusion, will perhaps frequently have to struggle with feelings of strangeness and aukwardness: they will look round for poetry, and will be induced to enquire by what species of courtesy these attempts can be permitted to assumed that title. It is desirable that such readers, for their own sakes, should not suffer the solitary word Poetry, a word of very disputed meaning, to stand in the way of their gratification: but that, while they are perusing this book, they should ask themselves if it contains a natural delineation of human passions, human characters, and human incidents; and if the answer be favourable to the author's wishes, that they should consent to be pleased in spite of that most dreadful enemy to out pleasures, our own pre-established codes of decision.

Readers of superior judgment may disapprove of the style in which many of these pieces are executed it must be expected that many lines and phrases will not exactly suit their taste. It will perhaps appear to them, that wishing to avoid the prevalent fault of the day, the author has sometimes descended too low, and that many of his expressions are too familiar, and not of sufficient.

Bibliography

"Humanism and Its Aspiration" The New Humanist. 2003 <http://www.americanhumanist.org>

Abrams, M.H. A Glossary of Literary Terms. Bangalore: Eastern Press, 2003.

Abrams, M.H. and Harold Bloom, eds. The Norton Anthology of Literature. New York: W.W. Norton & Company, 1976.

Allison, Alexander W. and H. Barrows, eds. The Norton Anthology of Poetry. New York: W.W. Norton Corp. Ltd., 1983.

Atkins, J.W.H. Literary Criticism : Renaissance. London: Methuen and Co., 1957.

Babbitt, Irving. Democracy and Leadership. Massachusetts: Riverside Press, 1924.

Humanism. Massachusetts: Riverside Press, 1920.

Bragg, Raymond, "Humanist Manifesto-I". The Humanist. May-Jun, 1933 <http://www. americanhumanist.org>

Bush, Douglas. John Milton. London: Weiden Field and Nicholson, 1964.

Chaucer, Geoffrey. A Prologue to the Canterburry Tales. ed. E.W. Robinson. London: Oxford University Press, 1983.

Chaudhari, Sukanta. Infirm Glory: Shakespeare and the Renaissance Image of Man. London: Oxford University Press, 1981.

Coleridge, S.T. Biographia Literaria. ed. J. Shawcross. London: Oxford University Press, 1962.

Cowell, Raymond. ed. Critics on Wordsworth. New Delhi: Universal Book Stall, 1990.

Daiches, David. From the beginnings to the sixteenth century, Vol 1. Bombay: Allied Publications, 1960.

De Burgh, W.G. The Legacy of the Ancient World Vol 2. Harmondsworth: Pelican Books Ltd., 1953.

Downey, James. "A Humanist Meets his waterloo". <http:/ /www. communications_uwaterloo_ca/gazette/1993>

James, Trevor. The Metaphysical Poets. Harlow: Longman, 1988.

Dunn, S.G., ed. William Wordsworth Select Poems. London; Oxford University Press, 1921.

Durant, Will. The Story of Philosophy. New York: Pocket Books Ltd, 1979.

Ford, Boris. From Dryden to Johnson. London: Penguin Publications Ltd., 1960.

Gandhi, Leela. Postcolonial Theory. New Delhi: Oxford University Press, 1996.

Gibaldi, Joseph. MLA Handbook for writers of Research Papers. New Delhi: East-West Press Pvt. Ltd., 2006.

Grierson, Herbert J.C. Milton & Wordsworth: Poets and Prophets. London: Cambridge University Press, 1937.

Harvey, W.J. and Richard Gravil, eds. The Prelude, A Casebook. London: The Macmillan Press Ltd., 1972.

Haveley, Cecily. Wordsworth. The Age of Revolutions. *Units 13-14*, Arts: A Second Level Course. Milton Keynes: The Open University Press, 1976.

Hope, Marjorie and Nicholson, eds. John Milton, A Reader's Guide to his Poetry. London: Thames and Hudson, 1964.

Jacobus, Mary. Tradition and Expriment in the Lyrical Ballads, *1798*. London: Clarendon Press, 1976.

Jones, R. and Tydeman, eds. William Wordsworth; Lyrical Ballads. London: The Macmillan Press Ltd., 1972.

Knight, Wilson. The Crown of Life. London: Oxford University Press, 1992.

Kurtz, Paul. "Humanist Manifesto-II" The New Humanist. Sep.-Oct., 1973 <http://www.americanhumanist.org>

Legouis, Emile and Louis Cazamian. History of English Literature. Trans. Helen Irvine. New Delhi : The Macmillan Ltd., 1987.

Legouis, Emile. The Early Life of Wordsworth 1770-1798:A Study of "The Prelude". Trans. J.W. Matthews. London: Oxford University Press, 1932.

Mackie, J.L. Problems from Locke. Oxford: Clarendon Press, 1976.

Marlowe, Christopher. Doctor Faustus. Ed. E. Robinson. Madras: The Macmillan Press Ltd., 1970.

Martin, A.D. The Religion of Wordsworth. London George Aleen & Unwin Ltd. 1936

Miller, Leo. F. History of Philosophy. New Delhi: Discovery Publishing House, 2002.

Milton, John. Paradise Lost I & II. ed. E.T. Prince. London: Oxford University Press, 1976.

O'Neill, Judth, ed. Critics on Jane Austen. New Delhi : Universal Book Stall, 1992.

Pope, Alexander. Collected Poems. ed. Bonamy Dobree. London: J.M. Dent & Sons Ltd., 1959.

Parrinder, Patrick. Authors and Authority. London: The Macmillan Press Ltd., 1980.

Patrick, G.T.W. Introduction to Philosophy. New Delhi: Surjeet Publications, 1980.

Perkins, David. Wordsworth and the Poetry of Sincerity. Masschusetts: The Belknap Press of Harvard University Press, 1964.

Pope, Bob. How to Study Chaucer. London: The Macmillan Press Ltd, 1988.

Rickert, Edith. Chaucer's World. Eds. Clair C. Olson. London: Geoffrey Cumberlege Oxford University Press, 1950.

Russell, Bertrand. The Principles of Philosophy. Bombay: Oxford University Press, 1986.

Saret, Jean Paul. Existentialism and Humanism. London: Oxford University Press, 1950

Shakespeare, W. The Tempest. Eds. Arthur Couch and Dover Wilson London: Cambridge University Press, 1965.

Edt. Shrivastava, S.B. An Anthology of English Literature. Bhopal: Madhya Pradesh Hindi Granth Academy, 2003.

Hamlet. ed. A.W. Verity. London: Cambridge University Press, 1966.

Macbeth. ed. J.R. Brown. London: Edward Arnold (Publishers) Ltd., 1967.

King Lear. Ed. A.W. Verity. London: Cambridge University Press, 1966.

Strunk, William. The Elements of Style. New York: The Macmillan Company, 1966.

Swannell, Julia, ed. The Modern Oxford English Dictionary. London: Oxford University Press, 1992.

Tillyard, E.M.W. Studies In Milton. London: Chatau and Windmus, 1960.

Vincent, Patrick. Review of Toby R. Benis's Romanticism on the Road: The Marginal Gains of Wordsworth's Homeless. New York: St Martin's Press, 2000. Online. <http:// users.ox.ac.uk/~scat0385/ 22benis.html>. 31 May 2004.)

Watson, J.R., ed. Pre-Romanticism in English Poetry of the Eighteenth Century. London: Macmillan Education Ltd., 1989.

Willey, Basil. The Eighteenth Century Background. London: Chatau and Windmus, 1957.

Wimsatt, William Jr. and Cleanth Brooks ed. Literary Critisim, a Short History. New York: Alfred A. Knopf, 1959.

Wordsworth, William. The Prelude. Ed. A.J. George. London: D.C. Heath & Company, 1930.

The Prelude. Ed. J.C. Maxwell. Hermondsworth: Penguin Books Ltd., 1972.

William Wordsworth Poetical Works. Ed. Thomas Hutchinson and Ernest De Selincourt. New York: Oxford University Press, 1987.

Poetical Works. Ed. Thomas Hutchinson. London: Oxford University Press, 1953.

General Virtue and Happiness, 30
Political Justice, 30
Goldsmith, Oliver, 44
Humanist in 'Deserted in Village', 44
Gray, Thomas, 43
Humanist, 43
Greek New Testament, 23
Guilt and Sorrow, 97, 98

H

Hawk Shead Grammer School, 47
Hugo, Victor, 47
Humanism, 16, 19, 20-22, 26, 31, 32, 37, 42, 44, 64, 67, 70, 82, 86, 94, 108, 109, 117
In England, 37
On Trial, 41
Traditional, 31
Humanist
Manifesto, 32, 33
Philosophers, 28
Jean Jacques Rousseau, 28
William Godwin, 28
Humanistic Religious Association, 31
Humanitarianism, 110, 115
Hume, David, 27
Huxley, Julian, 31

I

In the Waterfall and the Eglantine, 92
Irving, Babbi H, 31
Italian Ports, 22
Florence, 22
Padua, 22
Rome, 22
Venice, 22
Italian Scholars, 20

K

Kant, German Idealist, 51
King Edward III, 37
King Lear, 39

L

Locke, John, 26, 28, 29
John, Empiricism and Enlightenment Humanism, 26
Lucey Gray, 81
Lyrical Ballads (LB), 55, 57, 77, 94, 97
Humanism in -, 55, 81

M

Macbeth, 39
Maid of Buttermere, 132
Marlowe, Christopher, 38
Marxism, 16, 50
Milton, John, 23, 179, 181, 183
A Republican and Humanist, 107
Christian Humanist, 41

Liberal Humanist, 41
Renaissance Poet, 41

N

Natural
Sciences and Technology, 18
Socialism, 16
Netherlands, 22

O

Oppression and Injustice, 92
Optimist, Voltaire's Novel, 167

P

Paradise Lost, 41
Peel, Sir Robert, 51
Personalism, 16
Persons Who Influences Wordsworth, (PWIW), 50
Dorothy, 50, 51
Hannah More, 59
ST Coleridge, 51
Peter Bell, 99
Philosophical Humanism, (PH), 60, 67, 72, 88, 93, 101, 117
Philosophy
And Theology, 21
Lockian, 119
OF Rousseau and Godwin, 137
Natural, 18
Poetry and Moral, 18
Political, 29
Pitt and Burke, 142
Pragmatism, 19
Prelude, Humanism in-, 123-160
Pre-Romantic Poetry, 58

Q

Queen's Imperialist Policies, 182

R

Raymond, B Bragg, 32
Renaissance, 20, 21, 23, 25, 29, 37, 88, 107
Drama 39
Humanism, (RH), 18 RH, 24, 27, 28, 38, 41, 42, 67, 77, 88, 89, 103, 104, 106, 110-12, 114, 115, 117, 124, 126, 130, 149, 172, 176, 177
Republican Movement, 48
Return to Nature, 28
Revolutionaries, 48, 137
Richard II, 37
Rise of Naturalism, 31
Robert Burns's Poetry, 46
Roman Empire, 21
Romantic
Age, 50
Period, 31
Poets, 104
Romanticism, 43, 55

Rousseau, Jean Jacques, 29, 30, 38, 48
Rural Architecture, 88
Russell, Bertrand, 27

S

Salisbury Plain, 97, 98
Sartre, Jean-Paul, French Philosopher, 31
Science and Technology, 19
Shakespeare, William, 39
  Plays, 39
Shakespeare's As You Like It, 93
Sidney, Philip, Renaissance Humanist, 38
Simplon and Snowdon Incidents, 124
Spenser, Edmund, 38
Spinoza, 29
Stalinism, 16
Supernatural, 16, 17

T

Tale of an Old Huntsman, 77
The Female Vagrant, 97, 98
The Fountain, 84
The Tempest, 40, 182
Theology, 18
Tintern Abbey, 46, 49, 51, 67, 68, 94
Tolstoy, 92
Traditional Ballad, 61
Triumph of Modest Pride, 113

U

Utopia, 23

V

Valleys of Westermoreland, 115

W

Wanderer, 163, 164
Western Humanism, 16
Wilson, John, 61
Wordsworth, William, 15
  A Poet's Epitaph, Philosophical Humanism, 89
  As a Bolshevist, 179
  As Tory Humanist, 56
  Attack on Catholics, 89
  Crime of Life, 118
  Descriptive Sketches, 47
  Faith in Liberty, 110
  Favorite Poems, 61
  Favorite Poems, Idiot Boy, 61, 64
  Favorite Poems, The Thorn, 61, 64
  Humanism, 16, 57, 60, 64, 73, 83, 177
  Humanism in Shorter Poems, 97-120
  Humanism of Renaissance, 117

Humanist, 16
Humanitarian Instinct, 57, 67, 73, 83
Humanitarianism, 163
Letter as Communist Manifesto, 50
Life and Poetic Career, 46
Love for Animals and Trees, 157
Love of Nature, 67
Lyrical Ballads, 15, 58
Pet-Lamb, Pastoral, 82
Poems, 55
Poetry, 15, 29
Prelude-Greatest Poem, 123
Rejection of Rationalism, 119
Scorn for Monarchy, 139
Study of Sufferings, 98
Use of Stories of Grief and Destitution, 97
Views Against Tyranny, 119
Wife Mary Hutchinson, 51, 123, 146
Wordsworth Tintern Abbey, 15
World War II, 32